T0311752

THE SID KESS APPROACH

Sid

60 Years of
Best Practices
in Tax, Education,
Careers and Life

AICPA®

As told to James Carberry

Notice to Readers

The Sid Kess Approach: 60 Years of Best Practices in Tax, Education, Careers and Life does not represent an official position of the American Institute of Certified Public Accountants, and it is distributed with the understanding that the author and publisher are not rendering legal, accounting, or other professional services in the publication. This book is intended to be an overview of the topics discussed within, and the author has made every attempt to verify the completeness and accuracy of the information herein. However, neither the author nor publisher can guarantee the applicability of the information found herein. If legal advice or other expert assistance is required, the services of a competent professional should be sought.

Publisher: Amy M. Plent
Senior Managing Editor: Amy Krasnyanskaya

To my dear parents who sacrificed everything to give me and my brother and sister all that we needed, and who taught me the approach to life which I have been fortunate enough to be able to pass along to my children, grandchildren and great-grandchildren. I am sure that my parents would be very proud to see how the third and fourth generation are living their legacy.

—Sid

Foreword

In October 2011, the AICPA awarded its Gold Medal for Distinguished Service to a CPA by the name of Sid Kess. Kathy Eddy, who presented the award, noted that for 99.9% of the people in the room, Sid required no introduction. What she didn't mention was that this was probably also true for 99.9% of rest of the CPAs in the country.

It is hard to imagine a CPA who has touched as many of his colleagues lives, in such an impactful way. Sid has lectured before over 700,000 people in his career. I am one of them. If you count the others who haven't seen him in person but have read his books, taken a self-study or online course, or viewed a webcast, the number with whom he has shared his knowledge easily tops a million. But these numbers, though impressive, simply don't do justice to Sid's accomplishments. Because it's not so much about how many he taught as it is about what he taught us.

Before the age of electronic research, Sid insisted on traveling to speaking engagements with about 5 suitcases full of research guides. He wanted to be able to answer any question asked by a participant. He is famous for giving out his phone number from the podium and making himself available before, during and after the program for consultation and advice. Unlike many veterans of the speaking circuit, Sid never seems to grow weary of interacting with his audience. He gets to know the CPAs he meets. He knows our spouses' names, our kids' names. He is interested in our challenges, and he shares his ideas and solutions with stupendous generosity.

Sid knows a lot about tax strategy and planning. But he knows even more about relationships, and the value and importance of interpersonal connection. Sid taught a lot of us how to build strong connections with our clients, by the example he set in the way he connected with us.

Back when I was in practice in Buffalo, New York, me and 4 other members of my firm used to pile into a car and head down to Philadelphia to attend Sid's presentations. We called ourselves the "Sid Kess Groupies." Sid was a CPA rock star. He still is.

I am honored and proud that the AICPA is able to bring you this book, in which so many professionals who learned their trade from Sid share those experiences and the knowledge they gained. After all of these years Sid is still a font of ideas, and many of those ideas are here for you in these pages.

—Jim Metzler, CPA, CGMA, CITP
Vice President, Small Firm Interests
AICPA

About the Author

James Carberry is the principal of Carberry Communications, a business writing and editing service based in Portland, Oregon. He has been a corporate writer and editor, a business writer based in Singapore, and, for ten years, a staff reporter of the *Wall Street Journal*. Before joining the *Journal*, he was a reporter for newspapers in Berkeley and Riverside, California. Carberry is the co-author of *The Inside Track to Careers in Accounting*. He is a graduate of the University of Missouri School of Journalism.

Sid

Preface

The AICPA approached me in 2011 saying that they were going to ask CPAs to submit "Sid Kess stories," letters that would describe how I've had an influence on their lives. Many sent in touching letters, and they are featured in this book about my impact on many in the accounting world over the past half century. When I reviewed some of what was submitted, certain patterns and premises stood out that have exemplified my life. Upon reflection, I believe that these underlying principles have helped me become successful in my life and can help assure success to others.

I grew up during the Great Depression in a two and a half-room apartment, with a father who was often out of work. My parents insisted that their three children focus on achieving excellence, both at school and in the community. Quality education is where much of my success started. I took a number of years off to fight in WWII, then went to college and Harvard Law School upon my return from overseas.

Quality education must continue throughout life if one is to achieve success. Don't be satisfied with mediocrity in life, generally, or in your career, in particular. Read, research, take classes, attend conferences. Gain experience. Then, specialize! Develop your own area of personal excellence and expertise. Write about what interests you. Show that you have a breadth and depth of knowledge. Participate on panels. Speak at workshops, conferences. Become an expert and you will get recognized.

Be imaginative. Be an idea person. Think out of the box. Think locally and think globally: What do people care about? What do you care about? Teach. I've taught over 750,000 students! Teaching helps you give back to the profession and helps you build a professional reputation. You will also get exposure to prospective clients. It doesn't matter how old you are; if you are up-to-date and innovative, others will be interested in hearing from you.

Relationships matter. Don't forget to reach out. Put people first. Surround yourself with successful people, and you will all benefit. You will cultivate friendships and business associates. Go out of your way to lend a helping hand, to network and bring remarkable people together to build relationships and change the world. Decide who you want to help: Your profession? Your community? Then go for it. I have gotten more pleasure from my Rolodex than I would have ever gotten from a Rolex. I have developed a network so vast that there isn't a day when my phone is silent, not a day that I'm not worried about someone or celebrating another's triumph. I wouldn't have it any other way! For me, this is a successful life: *Take care of the people who matter to you, and matter to the people who take care of you.*

Also, think about giving to the less fortunate. Why do I focus on helping people? When I was a youngster growing up in poverty during the Depression, I learned how important a possible job opening or interview can be to a family. I have not forgotten that lesson. Pay it forward. Everyone should be sensitive, especially in today's economic climate, to the importance of helping those less fortunate at every level of life. Care. I don't just tip the skycap at the airport; I know his name, that his mother is ill, that his first wife died of cancer. It takes a minute, but it makes him smile.

Could it be that this is the "Sid Kess approach?" People have their own goals, and I don't suggest that others follow my approach just because it has worked for me. But I do suggest that if you care about others and try to help others, you will succeed beyond your greatest aspirations, because relationships matter. It's not complicated. I didn't learn this at Harvard. It's not a big secret you've never heard before. In fact, I believe you already know this to be true: *Success in life is all about successful relationships.* I delight in seeing kindness and sensitivity in my children and grandchildren and in my extended family and circle of friends.

I was not completely satisfied striving for the American definition of success with my conferences, books, workshops, videos, and scholarships. What does it mean to live successfully with the "Sid Kess approach?" Do you wake up each day and ask yourself, who can I help today? If you hear a person's troubling story, do you find it difficult to sleep at night until you figure out some small way to make it better for that person? Are you perpetually acting as a matchmaker, bringing people you know together with other people you know, so that everyone wins? Do you always remember the goodness that was done for you, and feel the happiest when you've made a difference in someone's life? That's my approach: Lend a helping hand and over deliver to the people you care about. Bring remarkable people together who can make a difference.

Go out of your way to express your gratitude. We use the expression "my right arm" to refer to people who have been so valuable to us, we couldn't have managed without them. Well, I have at least twenty right arms! I won't try to name them all here, because then I might leave out someone important. I must mention my secretaries, Mary Mora DeMaria, Sherry Eisner, Cecilia Anthony, and Rose Ann Beni, who have helped me in all capacities in my office; Joe Stein who worked with me for years on various newsletters; Joe Lobel, Don Korn, Florence Ditz, and Florence Malin; Marty Edelston, who is Chairman of Bottom Line Personal; Jim Cheeks, who updated my workshops with me for over twenty five years and ultimately became executive vice president, publisher and editor in chief of Thomson Reuters, previously known as RIA; Barbara Weltman who has coauthored many books with me and is today one of the leading small business advisors in the United States; and more names than there is room for in this book.

I must mention the AICPA. For over fifty years I have devoted many waking hours to the AICPA, a phenomenal organization that has contributed so much value to our profession. I see that joining this organization gives its members tremendous value for their money. I've enjoyed the same quality of experience with my publisher, CCH, over many years, and I appreciate the way that they were able to shape my ideas into new products for the profession.

At this point, some may wonder why I am not retired—why do I go on doing the things I do? "Retirement" isn't something I generally think about. In fact, I am now of counsel to Kostelanetz & Fink, LLP, one of the leading law firms in America representing clients with tax controversies and complex civil and white collar criminal issues. In essence, I have begun a new career! The point is— if you still "have it," continue to contribute your knowledge. You, and the world, will be better for it.

If you are lucky like me, you will live long enough to see your legacy unfold and to witness your children and grandchildren living fulfilling lives of service. People will greet you with a smile and a thank you, and you will know, at the end of the day, that you have done much and tried hard to create a masterpiece.

Contents

Chapter 2. Build and Maintain Core Knowledge and Expertise 19

Chapter 3. Be Imaginative and Act on Your Ideas 53

Contributors

Cecilia Anthony

Jim Avedisian, CPA

William Behrenfeld

Rose Ann Beni

Lenny Berk, CPA

Andrew Biebl, CPA
Principal LarsonAllen, LLP

Clark Blackman
Founder and President, Alpha Wealth
Strategies, LLC

Blanche Lark Christerson
Managing Director, Deutsche Bank, NY

John Connors
President, Tax Educators Network

E. Martin "Marty" Davidhoff
E. Martin Davidhoff & Associates

Fran Davis

David S. De Jong, LL.M., CPA
Principal, Stein Sperling Bennet De
Jong Driscoll

Jeremiah Doyle
Senior VP, BNY Wealth Management

Martin S. Finn
Founding Partner, Lavelle & Finn, LLP

Owen G. Fiore
FioreWealthPlanningConsulting

Jonathan Gassman
Managing Partner, Gassman &
Golodny, LLP

Seymour Goldberg, CPA
Goldberg & Goldberg P.C.

Stanley Goldstein, CPA

Carol Gonnella
Founder, Gonnella Anderson

Joe Gornick
Senior Manager of CCH Seminars

Art Grasso
Counsel, Chuhak & Tecson

R. Thomas Herman

Rachel Hirschfeld
PetTrustLawyer

Linda Hughes

Azriela Jaffe

Chith Kala, CPA

Martin L. Kamerow, CPA

Inky Kim
VP of Development, Futures for
Children

Robert S. Keebler
Partner, Keebler & Associates

Karen Koch, CPA
Partner, Bedford Cost Segregato

Lynn Kopon
Managing Editor, CCH

Bernard A. Krooks
Litman Krooks LLP

Beatrice Lemlin
KPMG

Gary Lesser
GSL Galactic Publishing

Charles R. Levun
Partner, Levun, Goodman & Cohen,
LLP

Joseph D. Mach

Harry A. Mervish, CPA

Robert Metz

Andrea Millar, CPA/PFS
Senior Technical Manager, PFP
Section, AICPA

Mike Miller, CPA
Concannon, Miller & Co. P.C.

Sondra Miller
Chief Counsel to McCarthy Finger,
LLP

Cecil Nazareth
Managing Partner, IFRS Partners

L. Paden Neeley, CPA

Karen A. Notaro
Portfolio Managing Editor, CCH

Kurt G. Oestriecher, CPA
Partner, Oestriecher and Company

Mariette O'Malley, CPA
Partner, O'Malley & O'Malley

Oscar Ornelas

Richard Oshins
Oshins & Associates, LLC

Jacqueline A. Patterson
Partner, Buchanan and Patterson

Mark Plostock, CIA, CITP

Walter S. Primoff
Director, Professional Advisor Group

Doug Puckett, CPA

Charles Rettig
Hochman Salkin Rettig Toscher &
Perez

Dina Reznichenko

Scott Rhine, CPA
Hinkle, Richter & Rine, LLP

Jan Rosen
Financial writer, *New York Times*

Helena Rosenwasser

Eliana Sachar, CPA

Ted Sarenski
President, Blue Ocean Strategic
Capital

Gerard H. Schreiber, Jr, CPA
Schreiber & Schreiber

Gary Scopes

Art Seltzer, CPA

Martin Shenkman, CPA

Perry Schulman, CPA

James A. Seidel
Director of Federal Tax Content,
Thomson Reuters

Steve Siegel, LL.M.
President, The Siegel Group

Bryan C. Skarlatos
Kostelanetz & Fink, LLP

Lee Slavutin

Ed Slott, CPA

Houston D. Smith, Jr
Robins, Eskew, Smith & Jordan

David M. Spitzberg
The CPA Firm of David M. Spitzberg

Elliot D. Stein, CPA

J. Paul Stockwell, CPA
Owner & Manager Stockwell &
Company

Calvin Swinson, CPA

Arthur J. Thielen, CPA
Maginnis Knechtel & Mcintyre, LLP

Carolyn R. Turnbull
Director of Tax, Moore Stephens
Tiller LLC

Joseph Walloch, CPA
Walloch Accountancy Corporation

Eli Weinberg
Treasurer, The Teagle Foundation

Julie Welch
Parnter, Meara Welch Browne, P.C.

Barbara Weltman

Alan S. Zipp, CPA

Introduction

Purpose of This Book

When you meet Sidney Kess, you know you have just met someone extraordinary. He is described throughout this book by several people as a *mensch*, a Yiddish word that literally means "human being," but figuratively, is a person who possesses integrity and honor, someone who does the right thing. It is because he embodies these very important qualities that he has become so successful not only in life, but also in his career.

Using Sid's own words and the tributes of others, this book describes his life and work in a way that will allow the reader access to the successful "Sid Kess Approach."

This book is intended to address the following questions:

- Why has Sid been so successful as a tax expert, practitioner, communicator, teacher, and mentor?

- What ideas and practices has he developed that have particular value today?

- What lessons can practicing CPAs, other professionals in similar fields, and students learn from him?

By exploring these questions, this book examines the Sid Kess Approach to business development, managing a practice, career management, developing expertise, collaboration, practice development, and giving back to the profession and society.

Each chapter draws on Sid's experience and observations, as well as those of practitioners he has taught, mentored, or worked with. Together, they offer suggestions about how practitioners can apply Sid's approach in their professional and personal lives.

For example, with Sid's guidance and support

- Jonathan Gassman's CPA firm diversified into financial planning services. (p. 26–27)

- Ed Slott applied what he learned in Sid's tax workshops to build his business. (p. 74–77)

- Kathy Koch, CPA, made a career change from public accounting to being a consulting expert in tax incentives for energy efficient buildings. (p. 32)

- Cecil Nazareth, CPA, became a recognized leader in International Financial Reporting Standards (IFRSs) and is now managing partner of IFRS Partners, a New York firm that provides education, training, and consulting in IFRSs. (p. 31–32)

- David De Jong, LL.M., CPA, principal, Stein Sperling Bennett De Jong Driscoll PC, Rockville, Maryland, began his career listening to Sid's tapes of new tax developments. Now, he looks back on many years as a speaker at Sid's workshops. (p. 98)

Important Themes

From Sid's life and career, and from the experiences of those he has known, worked with, and helped, some important themes emerge:

- **The power of ideas.**

  Throughout his career, Sid has constantly offered ideas, such as suggesting to an employer that it use a clearer, more appealing name on its magazine, creating a probability chart of questions most likely to be asked on a CPA exam, and suggesting ideas to tax practitioners about how their clients could minimize their taxes, plan their estates, or manage their businesses. As Sid has demonstrated, CPAs and other professionals have an edge in gaining recognition for their talents, competing for clients, and advancing in their careers when they offer creative, innovative ideas and convince others of the value of their ideas.

- **The power of communication.**

  As Sid's career has shown, CPAs and other professionals who can communicate in innovative ways can build their reputations, advance into leadership positions in their companies and their professions, and succeed in winning clients. Ways for CPAs to communicate innovatively include teaching workshops, leading presentations, and writing articles. CPAs will need not only strong technical skills but equally strong communication skills.

- **The importance of lifelong learning.**

  Increasing complexity and accelerating change in business, information technology, accounting, tax, and other areas require CPAs and other professionals to dedicate themselves to lifelong learning. Some ways to continue learning after one's formal education are through degree and certification programs, continuing professional education (CPE) courses, workshops, and independent study. CPAs who are at the forefront of learning will have an edge in the marketplace.

- **The need for expertise.**

  As Sid has noted, CPAs must have a solid grounding as generalists, with a thorough knowledge of accounting and business; however, that is not enough in an increasingly complex world. CPAs should consider developing expertise and building their reputations as experts. Some current areas of specialization with growing demand are financial planning, forensic accounting, IFRSs, state and local taxes, and health care.

- **More opportunities for business development.**

  Sole practitioners and CPA firms are finding more opportunities to grow their businesses by offering specialized services, such as estate planning, in addition to traditional tax or other services. With these opportunities come challenges, such as deciding which services to provide based on market demand, the ability of a firm to deliver particular types of services, and the investment in people and resources a firm must make to grow its business.

- **Increasing demand for CPE teachers.**

  The explosion of knowledge, the increasing complexity of business and accounting, and the need for expertise are some factors that suggest that demand for CPE teachers who are highly knowledgeable in their specialties and who have strong communication skills will continue to increase. To help meet this need, Sid has been identifying and training CPAs and other professionals as teachers and bringing them into the CPE lecture circuit by way of the workshops and conferences that he and others conduct. Professional organizations, such as the AICPA, are conducting training programs for professionals preparing to become CPE teachers. Current teachers, following Sid's leadership, are helping recruit the next generation of teachers. These efforts will be necessary to meet demand.

- **More collaboration among firms.**

  More small and medium-sized CPA firms are collaborating through CPA firm associations and networks to leverage their talents and resources, share knowledge, meet the demands of clients for global services and expertise, realize efficiencies in marketing and delivering services, and achieve other goals. To stay competitive, other firms should be encouraged to join or create their own networks.

- **The value in helping others.**

Sid has long encouraged CPAs and other professionals—indeed, everyone he knows—to reach out and help others find jobs, advance in their careers, develop expertise, start or expand businesses, become CPE teachers, and otherwise be successful. If people heeded his advice, the effect could be exponential: more people doing more good for more people.

- **More outreach to high school students.**

More demand for accounting services, the breadth of services offered, the need for expertise, and many other factors are creating a growing need for the best and brightest students to choose accounting as a career. Accounting firms face strong competition from other professions, corporations, and businesses for the top talent. Some firms and accounting organizations are reaching out to high school students and teachers to inform them about the career opportunities in accounting, sponsor programs for students to be mentored by CPAs, visit firm offices, and participate in other accounting-related activities. In particular, firms and organizations are working to interest more minority students in accounting and to assist them in enrolling in, and completing, accounting programs in college.

As you read this book, you will see that Sid has made innumerable contributions in all these areas, and his commitment to doing the right thing and helping others is a constant theme not only in his professional life, but also in his personal life. His approach to life and career is inspirational and should be mirrored by all professionals who want to make a difference in their field as well as in the lives of those they serve.

Sid

1

Truly Put People First

"Put people first." It's a familiar theme, often used in business, education, government, the not-for-profit sector, and, indeed, throughout our society. We hear "We put our customers first," or "We put our students first." But what does it mean to truly put people first? Sid has shown what it means in his devotion to his family; in his helping hundreds of people, from longtime friends to new acquaintances; and in his leading or contributing to many educational, community service, and professional organizations. He helps others not only out of a sense of moral obligation but also because in it he finds personal fulfillment. "Put people first" is his approach to living, manifested in his desire to help people learn, grow, and succeed. It is an example and a challenge for all. Just like Sid, you can use your talent, energy, and resourcefulness to help others, if you really try.

Sid Kess: Life and Career

Sid grew up in Brighton Beach, Brooklyn during the Depression, in a loving but poor family. His father, Irving, mother, Rose, sister, Sylvia, and brother, Charles, shared a small 2½ room apartment. His parents slept in a fold out bed in the living room. Having enough money for the rent was a constant worry. Irving was employed by various small accounting firms, assisting with audit work during the day and, during busy season, doing tax returns at night. Like other employees, he was promised overtime pay at the end of busy season, but the pay was meager compared with the long hours worked. "There was terrible exploitation at the time," Sid said.

Irving never had a formal college education, but he took correspondence courses in law, and he encouraged his son to go to college and study accounting, tax, and law. At a young age, Sid resolved that he would never exploit anyone. He would treat people fairly and with respect, and he would do what he could to help people. As it turned out, he would do a lot. At a young age, Sid demonstrated the originality, creativity, organizational skills, compassion, and boundless energy that are integral to his character.

Formative Years

High School

Sid attended Abraham Lincoln High School in Brooklyn. He won accolades from his principal, teachers, and advisors and graduated third in a class of 526 pupils. In later recommending him for an Army officer's training program, Joseph R. Orgel, Dean of Boys, said of Sid: "He has considered high school not only as a place where he was to master subjects of study that would prepare him for life outside but also as one that trains pupils to assume obligations and responsibilities as a good school citizen."

Among his many activities, Sid was president of his class, captain of the Dean's office, and president of the General Science, Current Events, and Movie Appreciation clubs. Sid's service wasn't confined to his school. World War II was being fought, and he formed a community council of various schools, churches, and civic organizations to sell defense bonds and otherwise support the war effort. His French teacher, Martha Kramer, was his favorite teacher, and they became lifelong friends. When she later had difficulty paying some medical bills, Sid paid them. He paid for an attendant at her nursing home. When she died, Sid took care of her burial. She is buried in the Kess family plot with Sid's mother and father.

Sid also was president of Arkon, the school's honor service society. Another of his favorite teachers, with whom Sid stayed in touch until the teacher's death at 100 years of age, was the faculty advisor of Arkon. Here are a few things that teacher wrote about Sid:

> My associations with him gave me great faith in the future of our world. While there are Sidney Kesses, we can be certain that all is not dark in this world. He wasn't the president of Arkon; he was half the organization. In the execution of his office, he went way beyond anything other incumbents had done. New forms and services were introduced by him, which prove that the boy is not only a

leader but a person of initiative. His character cannot be described. To realize what a man of character is, one need merely be in his company. This term was a memorable one for me because of my association with Sidney Kess.

College

Sid attended New York's Baruch College for one semester, but his education was interrupted by military service. He joined the U.S. Army Signal Corps and served in France and Germany. Returning home from the war, Sid resumed his studies at Baruch College, a part of The City College of New York. The G.I. bill and scholarships helped him to finance his undergraduate and, later, his graduate education, for which he has been forever grateful. "Only in America could a poor kid from Brooklyn go to the best schools," he said.

Just as in high school, Sid led, organized, and participated in many activities at Baruch College, among them, an orientation program for freshmen. He also was chancellor of the Sigma Alpha Honor Society. In recognition, the City College Student Council awarded him a Major Insignia for character, service, and scholarship. Two other students in Sid's class also received the award: Murray Weidenbaum, who became chief economic advisor to President Ronald Reagan, and Bernard L. Schwartz, who became chairman and CEO of Loral Space & Communications.

Sid graduated from Baruch in 1948. Baruch's dean of students later wrote to him, "You have a rare gift of creative leadership coupled with a feeling of personal responsibility for carrying through details. We in the college community will continue to profit from your devoted service for some time." Ross A. Baker, chemistry professor and faculty adviser to Sigma Alpha, wrote to Sid's parents "We only wish we could hold him here indefinitely, for he has an uncanny gift of keeping everybody around him working at top speed and, yet, happy at the same time."

Law School

Sid went on to Harvard, where he studied law. Most students were interested mainly in making big salaries working for top law firms. Doing pro bono work was almost unheard of. Sid set out to change that. He was president of the Law School Committee of Phillips Brooks House and, among his interests was getting students to engage in community service. He organized meetings of his fellow students and representatives of social agencies, not-for-profit organizations, religious institutions, to name a few, and they, in turn, pointed out how lawyers could get involved with communities to help solve problems. One such problem concerned a public health issue. Massachusetts state law mandated that cities require watertight garbage cans with covers to keep out rodents. The exception was Boston, where landlords, particularly those in the South End, didn't want to pay for the covers, claiming that people would steal them. The landlords were supported in that position by the administration of Boston's powerful mayor, James Curley. Despite the opposition, Sid and his committee were successful in persuading the city to pass a law requiring the lids. The committee went on to address other issues, such as providing legal aid for community organizations.

Sid also helped to found the Harvard Student Legislative Reference Bureau, whose student members prepared analyses of draft statutes that appeared in the *Harvard Journal on Legislation*. Founded in 1964, the journal publishes articles analyzing legislation and the legislative process. By 1969, the journal had expanded beyond the Legislative Reference Bureau to become a full scale law review, providing opportunities to write articles to students who were not staff members of the *Harvard Law Review*.

Shortly before graduating, Sid submitted a final report to the school on the activities and accomplishments of the Law School Committee. In a letter to Sid, Erwin N. Griswold, Harvard's dean, said "Not only is the report the best and most comprehensive of any that has been prepared during the past six years, but it reflects operations of the Law School Committee which have been far more extensive, far better planned, and far more effectively carried out than those of any of your predecessors since the War."

Sid also participated in other activities, such as organizing an orientation program for incoming freshman. At his suggestion, Harvard hosted a free dinner for the entire freshman class shortly before school opened. Livingston Hall, vice dean of Harvard, later wrote to Sid to thank him for his efforts. He also was active in The Institute for Social Progress at Wellesley College. The institute brought together people from all walks of life, among them Benjamin Graham, the famed stock market analyst.

Korean War Relief Effort

While Sid was at Harvard, the Korean War was being fought. He read that, upon his arrival in Korea to command UN forces there, General Matthew Ridgeway had said that the American people could not comprehend the plight of the Korean people. Some American troops reportedly were belittling Koreans because they were poor, looked different, or didn't speak English. Sid wrote a letter to President Truman suggesting that a committee of prominent U.S. citizens be formed to assist in alleviating the problems of the Korean people. Among other objectives, the committee could demonstrate America's compassion for the plight of Koreans by coordinating Korean relief efforts, including the shipment of food, clothing, and medicine to Korea. Sid also suggested that a Freedom Train travel the United States to raise contributions for the relief effort.

In reply, he received a letter from the U.S. State Department asking if he would like to help with the relief effort that was underway in the United States and suggested he contact American Relief for Korea, Inc., a New York based organization. Sid spent the summer providing pro bono service to this relief agency. From Harvard, Sid helped the organization raise donations for the relief of the people of the war torn country. After Sid had graduated from Harvard, Robert F. McGovern, the organization's administrative secretary, wrote a letter of reference for Sid, which stated "I have seen firsthand examples of his thorough working habits, his diligence, and initiative." He praised Sid for maintaining a high academic standing while serving as a leader of social and community programs.

Sid graduated from Harvard in 1952, and his parents, along with other members of Sid's family, attended the graduation ceremonies. Sid had achieved Irving's aspirations for him: to earn degrees in accounting and law.

Public Accounting

After graduating from Harvard, Sid joined Lybrand, Ross Brothers & Montgomery in the audit department. He wanted to work in tax, but he had to have two years of experience as an auditor to take the CPA exam. While working in audit, he passed three parts of the CPA exam, and after acquiring the requisite experience, he passed the fourth part. He also was going to school at night, studying for an LLM (master of laws) in taxation at New York University School of Law. He graduated in 1955.

While at Lybrand, Sid, as always, had ideas, one of which was that the firm could increase the promotional value of its magazine sent to clients and prospects by changing the magazine's name from LRB&M Journal to a simpler name: Lybrand Journal. "It was a simple change," Sid noted, "but sometimes we tend to overlook the obvious."

After Sid moved from Lybrand's audit to its tax department, he took some in-house tax courses. "The problem with these courses was that they were too legalistic," he said. "I suggested they change their approach from a focus on the tax code to more of an accounting approach." The firm liked the idea so well that they put him in charge of tax training.

Sid had ideas not only for Lybrand, but the profession itself. In 1954, he wrote a six-page letter to J.S. Seidman, president of the New York Society of CPAs. Among other recommendations, Sid suggested programs to encourage more active participation by accountants who were not yet certified, such as having open meetings on certain topics in addition to meetings open only to Society members, or considering a qualified membership with certain benefits for those who were waiting to meet the required three years to take the

CPA exam. In 1968, the Association of CPA Candidates acknowledged Sid's unselfish service and guidance to their organization.

In 1958, Sid wrote a memorandum to Alvin R. Jennings, managing partner of Lybrand, who had been elected to serve a term as (then) president of the AICPA. The memo included suggestions concerning improvement of an AICPA publication, achieving wider acceptance of accounting principles formulated by the AICPA, and the relation of the AICPA to the college student, non-CPA, and CPA candidate. Jennings forwarded Sid's letter to the AICPA's (then) executive director, John L. Carey, who replied to Sid. He said Sid's letter "shows that you have been paying attention to what the Institute has been doing and that you have done some original thinking about what it ought to be doing." He said he would have Sid's memo distributed to department heads and would discuss them at a staff meeting.

In 1969, Sid left Lybrand to join Main Lafrentz as national tax director. Through a series of mergers, the firm became KMG Main Hurdman, with Sid as national tax director. Later, Sid became a national tax partner with KPMG Peat Marwick. He retired from KPMG in 1988.

Importance of Family

In accepting the AICPA's Gold Medal award in 2011, Sid commented that "this medal is important, my family even more so." When his parents were alive, he called them every day, no matter how busy he was. "They didn't have the same opportunities that I did, and I wanted to share my life with them," he said. He also looked after his siblings. His brother Charles spent his career with the IRS, and his sister Sylvia was a teacher. He spoke with Charles every day until Charles passed away, and he speaks often with his sister. Sid has four adult children: a son, A.J., and three daughters, Deborah, Rachelle, and Sharon, as well as 13 grandchildren and three great-grandchildren. He often spends time with them and regularly talks to them on the phone.

Sid has this advice for other professionals concerning family matters: "thank your parents for all they have done for you; spend time with your family; treat them with respect; offer them help and support; celebrate their accomplishments; and treasure your moments with them. If you are divorced, for whatever reason, speak well of your former spouse and treat him or her with respect. This matters to your children more than you may know."

Learning From Sid

From his earliest days as a tax practitioner, speaker, teacher, writer, editor, and as an advisor and mentor, Sid has put into practice the values that are now institutionalized in the AICPA's Vision Statement, contained in its "The CPA

Vision Project: 2011 and Beyond." That vision statement says the core purpose of CPAs "is making sense of a complex world."[1] CPAs can accomplish this aim by

- communicating the total picture with clarity and objectivity;
- translating complex information into critical knowledge;
- anticipating and creating opportunities; and
- designing pathways that transform vision into reality.

The AICPA built on the CPA Vision Project to initiate a new project, CPA Horizons 2025, which extends that vision into the future. It is a roadmap for the profession.[2] Sid has not been involved in the 2025 project, but during his career, he has been working to advance the goals articulated in the project. For example, in the area of lifelong learning, the 2025 project report says that CPAs must devote more time to staying current with regulations and standards as well as with social, economic, technological, and political trends domestically and abroad. Sid has spoken at length with CPAs and others about the need to read and study, not just tax or other technical subjects, but broadly, in order to develop knowledge and insights.

By learning about Sid's life and career, CPAs can gain insight into how they can achieve their profession's goals articulated in the 2011 and 2025 vision projects, as well as their own professional and personal goals.

Honoring Sid

In 2011, the AICPA awarded Sid the AICPA Gold Medal Award, its highest honor, for his lifelong hard work, talents, and achievements. Kathy Eddy, chair of the awards committee and former AICPA chair, said that Sid and Scott Voynich, a fellow award winner, "have significantly contributed to the growth and success of the accounting profession and their communities throughout their distinguished careers." In 2010, the AICPA established the Sidney Kess Award for Excellence in Continuing Education to recognize individual

How Do You Learn From Sid?

Jeremiah Doyle is senior vice president at BNY Mellon Wealth Management in Boston:

How do you learn from Sid? You simply watch him and listen to him. You will learn how to present, how to market, how to network, how to communicate, how to separate the relevant from the irrelevant, and how to focus on the practical. You learn how to remain even-tempered and to always have a smile on your face. You learn that a lot can be accomplished by requesting something in a friendly, rather than a demanding, manner. Most important, you learn how to make lasting friendships in the profession. You will learn how to make learning enjoyable. He teaches by example.

---

1 "The CPA Vision Project: 2011 and Beyond," AICPA. www.aicpa.org/research/cpahorizons2025/cpavisionproject/downloadabledocuments/cpavisionproject_finalreport.pdf.
2 "CPA Horizons results will guide the profession through 2025," AICPA, www.aicpa.org/research/cpahorizons2025/pages/cpahorizons2025.aspx.

Sid's Remarks on Receiving the AICPA's Gold Medal Award

In his remarks upon receiving the AIC-PA's Gold Medal Award, Sid discussed how the world and the profession have changed since he began his career more than 50 years ago, reflected on the value of family and friends, and talked about future opportunities and challenges facing the profession. The following are some highlights of his remarks:

- Family and friends: "This medal is important to me, my family even more so. I am so blessed to have a wonderful family and so many friends. They are what life is all about."

- Only in America: "I grew up in a poor family during the Depression, and I have had an opportunity for the best education. Only in America could this have happened."

- Advancement of women: "More women are moving into leadership positions in the AICPA and the profession, and the profession must continue to make every effort to provide leadership opportunities for women."

- Center of learning: "The AICPA is a center of professional knowledge and learning. Because of advances in technology, the Institute can easily share information with members, and members can share among them-selves and at a fraction of the cost compared with 20 or 30 years ago."

- Wealth of knowledge: The Institute has a wealth of knowledge and information of tremendous value. "If you've attended any of the Institute's conferences, you know it has a

CPAs who have made significant and outstanding contributions in tax and financial planning and whose public service exemplifies the CPA profession's finest values and ethics. Sid was the first recipient.

Also in 2011, CCH gave its first Lifetime Achievement Award to Sid. The National Association of Estate Planners and Councils elected Sid to The Estate Planning Hall of Fame and gave him its 2009 Hartman Axley Lifetime Achievement Award. The New York State Society of CPAs named him to its Hall of Fame. "Sid is a living legend for all practitioners in the fields of tax and financial planning," Perry A. Shulman, CPA, said in endorsing his nomination to the New York Society's Hall of Fame."[3]

A Good Guy

As his many friends and admirers will attest, Sid is a good guy.

Jacqueline A. Patterson, a partner with Buchanan and Patterson, a Los Angeles law firm, said "When I think about Sid, my heart fills up with joy and gratitude for knowing him, working with him, and learning from him. Sid always takes time for all of us and is the first to lend a hand and give a good word. He never quits learning or participating and stays directly on the pulse of what's new and helpful. He is the best!"

Carol Gonnella, founder of Gonnella Adamson, a Jackson, Wyoming law firm, said "To sum Sid up in two words: he cares. He cares about our professional lives, and he cares about our personal lives. He wants to help all those he meets to have

---

3   "William Donaldson, CPA, JD and Sidney Sid, CPA, JD, Named to NYSSCPA Hall of Fame," press release, New York Society of CPAs, March 17, 2009, www.nysscpa.org/society/PR/3-17-09releasea.htm.

meaningful, significant, professional careers and loving, personal relationships."

Motivator

Robert S. Keebler, CPA, an estate planning attorney in Green Bay, Wisconsin, said this of Sid: "Many people recognize only Sid's gift of vast intellect and his ability to 'see around corners.' However, those who know Sid admire and respect him for being such a fine person and a good friend, with an incredible ability to motivate others."

The Professional's Professional

Charles Rettig, a tax lawyer with the Beverly Hills firm of Hochman Salkin Rettig Toscher & Perez, observed "Every interaction with Sid begins with 'How can I help you?' From there, Sid proceeds to inquire about your family, practice, and life in general. Sid is the professional's professional."

Practical Advice

Many of Sid's friends and colleagues have looked to him for advice not only on professional matters but on personal issues as well. John Connors, president of the Tax Educators' Network in Mequon, Wisconsin, said "On a practical level, Sid has always emphasized to let things go, even when someone has perhaps treated you unfairly, professionally or from a personal standpoint. Just move on and learn from the experience and never seek any form of retribution."

goldmine of material. It is tremendously valuable, and I hope it can be tapped and put to greater use."

- More learning opportunities: "The AICPA offers more learning opportunities than ever. It conducts more than 53 conferences on tax and other topics as well as CPE classes, webinars, and much more."

- Rise of the experts: "At one time, public accounting firms consisted mainly of generalists who knew everything. Today, that would be impossible. Accounting is so complicated that there are experts in many areas, such as valuation, not-for-profit, estate planning, and state and local government."

- More aggressive recruiting of talent: "The profession has accelerated its efforts to recruit, train, and advance the next generation of leaders, and it must continue to do so. We need to recruit outstanding people in accounting—and with the same intensity as sport teams or computer companies going after the best talent."

- Final thought: "Although demand for CPAs is strong, that is not the case in much of the rest of the job market. Unemployment is high, and CPAs can do a valuable service in helping others find work. They can talk to their clients to see if they have a need for people and connect them with people who might qualify. We can perform a valuable service for the unemployed, for the economy, and for America by opening doors to possible jobs."

A History of Helping

In high school, college, and throughout his professional career, Sid has given back to society through public service; to the profession, through teaching and other volunteer activities; and to those in need of guidance, support, or simply a kind word.

This section illustrates Sid's passion for helping others:

Individuals

• *Joe Lobel, an attorney and former editor of the* Tax Fortnighter, *published by Matthew Bender.* "He also wrote a brilliant book on corporate reorganizations," Sid said. When Lobel lost his editing job, "I helped him get a job at Lybrand Ross Brothers," Sid said, adding that "it was at the starting salary because they were not anxious to hire anyone." Lobel ultimately became one of the top people in Lybrand's National Tax Research Department.

• *Joe Stein, a high school friend, who graduated from Columbia Law School.* Stein worked on estate planning material for the Institute of Business Planning (IBP), a company owned by William J. Casey. When Casey, who had served in the Office of Strategic Services in World War II, became the head of the CIA during the Reagan administration, he terminated his relationship with IBP, and Stein was out of work. "I helped him get a legal position at Met Life," Sid said. "Joe helped develop with me the *CCH Estate Planning Review*, the estate planning courses, and the *Financial and Estate Planning Reporter*. When he passed away, his children said if they ever have a problem, Joe's last words were to contact Sid."

• *Arthur Rosenfeld, a Harvard Law School graduate and attorney, who became a leading publisher in the field of professional reference publishing.* Sid recalls, "I brought Arthur into the publisher Warren Gorham & Lamont as a vice president. Arthur became president of WG&L, and he made the company one of the leading textbook publishers in America." Rosenfeld went on to become president of Prentice-Hall Tax & Professional Reference Publishing and, later, president of Maxwell Publishing, which took over Prentice-Hall.

• *Pat Verde, an elevator starter in Rockefeller Center.* One day, when Sid got on the elevator to go to his office, he said, "Pat, you look very sad." Pat replied, "Sid, as you know, I am going through a very difficult divorce, and I just couldn't

---

Why the Bellman Refused a Tip

Houston D. Smith, Jr., CPA/PFS, is a partner emeritus with Robins, Eskew, Smith & Jordan, Atlanta. He and Sid had attended a meeting at the AICPA headquarters at the Harborside Financial Center in Jersey City, New Jersey and planned to share a cab to New York. Sid asked the bellman, Placido, to retrieve luggage he had stored the night before.

"Sid, never known for light packing, had enough boxes of books to start a CPA firm's library," Smith said. "Placido cheerfully packed the cab's trunk, filling it to overflowing. Sid offered him a gratuity. Placido said, 'No...no...Mr. Kess.'" He turned to Smith and said, "Mr. Kess...he treats me like...my...papa!"

"A small miracle had happened. I had seen a hotel bellman refuse a tip! But a greater miracle had also happened. I had gained an insight into Sid's greatness—he treats everyone he meets as if that person was the most important person he'd ever met. It does not matter how humble that person's occupation or station in life...he or she is a divine creation and worthy of respect.

afford to have my lawyer come with me when I was meeting with the judge. When I went to the judge's office, the judge would not talk to me unless I had someone accompany me." Sid told Pat that he would go with him, but he had to recognize that Sid was not a New Jersey attorney or a matrimonial lawyer. His field was taxation, and he had never been to court. The next week, Sid accompanied Pat to the judge's chambers and, to Pat's amazement, the judge said to Sid, "What are you doing here? I attended one of your programs." From that point on, the tone of the hearings changed completely.

Pat never forgot the favor. In Sid's office is a Seiko clock inscribed, "To my friend Sid Kess. Thank you for your valuable time. Pat. 8/17/89." Pat invited Sid, along with his family and children, who he had not seen for years, to an old-fashioned Italian restaurant on Mulberry Street in New York City. Pat has since passed away, but his children called Sid to let him know what he meant to their dad.

The "Dream Team"

Inky Kim is vice president of development of Futures for Children, a not-for-profit organization based in Albuquerque, New Mexico.

Their mission is to enhance the quality of the educational experience for American Indian students through mentoring and leadership development. It has a youth leadership program that helps children to develop leadership skills, a mentoring program that matches children with mentors across the United States, and a program to help families and students overcome barriers to success.

I had the great honor of meeting Sid in 1999 during my tenure as a Major and Planned Gifts officer at his alma mater, Baruch College. We worked on the fifth annual Conference on Estate Planning together. Each year, his name, alone, pulled in over 100 top CPAs in New York City to attend the conference.

After I left Baruch College, Sid remained my friend and mentor. He played a tremendous role by being a guide for all the charitable organizations and projects I worked for in New York City, including the Alvin Ailey Capital Campaign and Action Against Hunger, and always provided great ideas.

Sid Kess was key in getting my current position as vice president of development of Futures for Children based in Albuquerque, New Mexico. Sid currently chairs the Futures for Children DreamMaker Legacy Circle Dream Team (our new planned giving society). He was instrumental in gathering leading CPAs and estate attorneys across the country to be on this "dream team." He does this because he cares about Futures for Children, American Indian children, and all of humanity.

Sid Kess is a *mensch!* He is a dream maker for all those who are lucky to have met him.

Sid is also an idea guru, a door opener to the legal and accounting professions, and kind enough to connect them to the folks in the non-profit world, like me, to create a world filled with sharing and giving.

I am forever grateful that Sid is my friend and mentor. The world is a better place, because of Sid. I am lucky, indeed!

"I'm a better professional because of Sid Kess...and a better person"

Joe Gornick is Senior Manager of CCH Seminars at CCH, a Wolters Kluwer business.

Sidney Kess is legend among legends, certainly for his classes, his teaching, his publications, and his many other work products. But, that does not fully reflect, by any stretch of the imagination, Sid's many, many contributions to the profession and to the thousands of people's lives he has touched. You really need to address Sid Kess, the person, the man, to truly appreciate what makes him stand out among others in the tax and accounting professional community.

I have known Sid since my third day on the job with CCH, back in 1985. I had to call him about his annual Individual Income Tax Refresher course and get that product advertised and into production. I didn't really know what the product was or who Sid Kess was at that very early point in my career. But Sid graciously guided me then, not just with what I needed to do with this particular product, but with advice on getting started on a new job right out of college. And he has continued to help me, and a multitude of other CCHers, through the years.

When I think of Sid Kess, I think of sincerity, integrity, creativity, caring, compassion, kindness, dependability. In a word, he's amazing. He's like a tax profession superman. Although he may be some five-and-a-half feet tall, he's really head-and-shoulders above anyone I have ever met. I hold Sid—and, indeed, everyone else who knows him—in the highest regard, in a class by himself.

He's a guide, a coach, a mentor, a friend. He's a family man—and he has taught me and reminded me countless times about what is *the most* important thing in life, your family. He talks with his kids every day. While his dear mother was alive, he talked to her all the time and checked in on her every day to make sure she was okay. But for Sid, his "family" is bigger than his immediate family. It's all of us—all of those who have had the honor of knowing Sid and working with him over the years. I know that I consider myself part of Sid's family. And he treats me that way too. He's like a second father to me. When Sid calls me, not a conversation goes by, no matter how brief, where he doesn't ask about my wife and kids. Sid does that, not out of politeness, but it's because he *really* cares.

In addition to all that, Sid is also an idea man who is willing to share his insights and ideas. He's an "idea machine." I wish I had a dollar for every idea Sid has shared with me, both professionally and for my life outside of work. I would be a very wealthy man with all the suggestions and tips he's given me.

A few years ago, Sid put on a seminar at CCH for all of our federal tax and estate planning editors at our headquarters. He talked about the importance of wills and trusts and retirement planning. But the real gem of his presentation was that Sid addressed and encouraged the individual editors to be the best professionals that they can; how they should prepare for their own retirement and get a good balance in their life; and how they can achieve more in life. It was a real heart-to-heart session that I will never forget. Sid has done that countless times over the years, in many venues, to the benefit of so many people.

When Sid says, "You can call me any time," he genuinely means it. We have had situations where customers have had questions about a publication or a CPE course that Sid wrote for us. Sid says, "Have the customer call me. I'm on the road now. Give them my number. I'm at such and such hotel." When the customers call him, he always takes the time to help them directly, treating each person with whom he interacts with dignity, respect, and care.

I am a better professional because of Sid Kess—and I'm a better person because of him. I am truly blessed to call Sid my mentor, my friend, my second father.

"Sid always brings genuine interest and curiosity, an open mind and a sharp intelligence."

Lynn Kopon is Managing Editor for Journals at CCH.

I first met Sid in Chicago, and I knew right away that he is that rare individual who naturally focuses on human dignity and respect. It is unusual to find people like this, and it was tremendously refreshing to meet Sid. I value our relationship and appreciate my good fortune in meeting him. Sid always brings genuine interest and curiosity, an open mind, and a sharp intelligence.

Sid is possibly the best continuing education planner of our time and has organized hundreds of professional tax conferences over the course of his career. Attending one of his conferences in Las Vegas, I could see that he was a super star among his peers. He is also a philanthropist and a visionary.

The first time I met Sid, he was chairing a high level estate planning advisory board meeting in Chicago. He opened the program, led the discussion, introduced the speakers, commented on the issues being discussed, and invited others to comment. At the break, I saw him go deliberately to the young man who was recording the session and invite him to have some dessert and refreshments. Although Sid was running the program, he was not too busy to notice that someone was not having cake, and so this also became his responsibility. It was a completely natural thing for Sid. He probably didn't even know he was doing it.

The second time I met Sid, he was visiting his publisher's headquarters to discuss business issues relating to his work as author and consulting editor. While he was there, he hosted an estate planning session. During this meeting, Sid presented basic estate planning advice, related some of his own experiences, and pointed out some simple steps that could be taken to avoid problems, protect families, and provide transitions. His advice was practical and of great value for these employees and their families. Even during a busy work and travel day, Sid took the time to share his expertise.

I had the opportunity to attend one of Sid's High Income conferences in Las Vegas one year. While there, some colleagues and I had dinner with Sid. We talked business and politics, world affairs, the financial crisis, families, and careers. Sid doesn't carry on a conversation through a filter of self-interest. He comes to the table willing to share his knowledge and experience, and he is interested in hearing about yours. This is why it is so great to know Sid Kess and why he is so loved by everyone he meets.

Of course, he is talented. His inherent qualities of openness and respect serve him well on all levels. People gravitate to this element of the genuine, and his professional success reflects this because of the great generosity of spirit that he brings. I like to be near it, and I can see that it attracts others.

At the Las Vegas conference, I was sitting in a large audience of around 600 people listening to the presenters. It was a crowded room. At the break, as Sid closed the session and walked off the stage to sustained applause, he came directly to where I was standing, took my arm and said, "Walk me to the elevator." How, I wondered, did he find me in that room? Why did he choose me to walk him to the elevator? How does he see everything that is going on in the room while running the entire show? How can he be eating chocolate cake one minute and addressing an audience of thousands the next? Why does he have such a generous spirit even to those he barely knows or does not know at all? These are some of the rare qualities of Sid Kess, and I am pleased to witness this charming and special person.

How Sid helped refugees from Russia

Dina Reznichenko:

One morning in March of 1982 my husband Felix and I were taking the Brighton Beach subway from Brooklyn to Manhattan. The train was packed; there was standing room only. I was reading an accounting textbook, and my husband was going through a stack of index cards that he had prepared the night before. This caught the attention of a gentleman standing next to us. He wanted to find out what my husband was studying.

We had arrived in New York as refugees from Russia just two months earlier. My husband was a prominent doctor in Russia for 20 years, treating children with leukemia. In order to continue to practice medicine in the United States he had to pass several medical exams and go through a medical residency training program. My husband used the index cards to study medical terms in English. The gentleman showed a great interest in our family, and when it was a time for us to get off the train, he took my accounting textbook and wrote his name and telephone number on the cover. He mentioned that we should not hesitate to give him a call if we needed any help. That was our first meeting with Mr. Sidney Kess.

At this point we were not familiar with the concept of the kindness of strangers and never called Mr. Kess. However, a few weeks later we were very surprised to receive a call from him. Mr. Kess wanted to know how we were doing. We mentioned that our older daughter was admitted to New York University and that my husband was studying hard for his first medical exam which was only two months away. After that Mr. Kess called us every two weeks to offer support and encouragement, which was very important to us. At that time we had neither relatives nor friends in this country.

At the end of August I completed my study in accounting and got my very first job in the United States as a bookkeeper. I kept my accounting textbook handy while at work. One day an accountant from the auditing firm showed up in the office and noticed my textbook with Mr. Kess's name and telephone number. He was very surprised and asked me if I knew Mr. Kess in person. As I told him the story about my meeting Mr. Kess on the subway train, the accountant became more and more amazed. I was really puzzled by his reaction. He finally told me that Mr. Kess is the Einstein of tax law.

My husband finally passed the required medical exams and was looking for a residency training program. Mr. Kess offered to review my husband's resume. Once it was completed, Mr. Kess sent it back to us along with 400 already stamped envelopes with the addresses of pediatric residency programs all over the United States. This was of tremendous help to us because of our limited finances.

In March of 1984, Mr. Kess called us at 5:00 a.m. one morning from Louisiana, where he was presenting an AICPA workshop, to congratulate my husband on his acceptance into a pediatric residency program at the Staten Island Hospital.

Three years later my husband became a licensed pediatrician in New York, where he opened his own practice and successfully worked for 23 years.

When our older daughter graduated from New York University, Sidney asked his wife Lydia to help her to find a job.

Over the years Mr. Kess became our mentor and a member of our family. He attended the wedding of our older daughter as well as my husband's 60th birthday party. He offered guidance to our younger daughter when she attended Columbia University.

We met Mr. Kess almost 30 years ago just as we came to the United States. For all those years Mr. Kess was a guiding light for us, and we are very honored to know him and to call him our dear friend. This miracle can happen only in America.

Organizations

UJA-Federation of New York

In 1969, when Sid became the national director of taxes at Main LaFrentz, the partner in charge asked Sid to talk to one of the officers of the UJA-Federation of New York and offer ideas about how the organization could reach accountants and lawyers. The UJA-Federation wanted to capitalize on the new Foundation rules (private foundation rules) that were enacted in the Tax Reform Act of 1969. In meeting with the officer, Sid recalled a UJA-Federation breakfast meeting he had attended years earlier. Those in attendance were asked to fill out pledge cards, and each person's pledge was read to the entire group. Sid said, "It's no one's business how much I am giving. If someone can only afford $25, rather than $1000, that's their affair." However, the officer said this technique had been most effective for the organization, and he asked Sid for an alternative. Sid had an idea about how the federation could improve its image in the community and raise money. He felt that most CPAs and attorneys had no formal training in estate and financial planning in their business, accounting, and law school curriculums. Sid suggested the UJA-Federation organize an annual conference on estate, tax, and financial planning. The UJA-Federation officer asked Sid if he would organize and moderate the program. Sid said, "On one condition—that there would be

Claflin University: Sid Talks to the Students About Paul Robeson

In February 2006, during Black History Month, Sid traveled to Orangeburg, South Carolina, to speak at a luncheon hosted by Claflin University's School of Business.

Founded in 1869, Claflin is a historically black liberal arts university affiliated with the United Methodist Church.

The university had asked Sid to speak on "The Impact of U.S. Tax Policy on the African American Community." Sid thought, "Who am I to speak on that topic? I had never given it any thought before." He was also asked to weave into his speech some thoughts about Black History Month, an annual event that recognizes the central role of black Americans in U.S. history and celebrates the achievements of African Americans.

What could he say about Black History Month?

Sid remembered that when he was attending Abraham Lincoln High School in Brooklyn he had presented the school's Lincoln Award for a lifetime of achievement to Paul Robeson, a famous African American actor, singer, recording artist, athlete, scholar, and civil rights activist.

Sid bought some of Robeson's CDs and picked out those he thought might interest Claflin students. He wanted to compile his selections on a single CD, so he asked for help from his grandson, a musician who has his own band and was in the process of recording a CD of religious Jewish music.

Sid's luncheon speech was attended by about 500 students and faculty. As they were assembling, they heard the CD of Robeson's songs over the speaker system. While the recording continued, Sid asked the students if they had heard of Paul Robeson. Not many had, but he had sparked their interest. Sid talked about Robeson's life and career and some his many achievements.

Born in 1898, Robeson was the son of a minister who had escaped from slavery, joined the Union Army and, after the Civil War, earned a divinity degree. His mother, a Philadelphia school teacher, was from a prominent

(continued on pg. 16)

(continued from pg. 15)

African American family. He was one of the first black students to attend Rutgers University, where he was an outstanding scholar and athlete. After earning a law degree from Columbia University, he joined a white law firm; but, at the time, it was impossible for a black person to represent clients in court, and he was relegated to researching briefs. When a secretary refused to take dictation from him, he put on his hat and walked out. To support himself in law school, Robeson had done some acting and singing. After he left a career in law, he began to appear on the New York stage, soon wining acclaim for his performances in *Othello* and other plays. He went on to perform as an actor and singer before audiences in the United States and Europe and in Hollywood films. He was an outspoken advocate of civil rights and social justice.*

After speaking about Robeson, Sid talked about U.S. tax law. Discrimination in the tax law is not so much a racial issue as it is an economic issue, he told the students. As an example, he noted that Congress (in 2006, when he was speaking) was considering cuts in Medicare that would have impacted millions of Americans at the same time it was also considering cuts in taxes on dividends and capital gains that would have favored investors.

Sid spent three days at Claflin, meeting with students, learning about their lives, their career aspirations, their hopes and dreams. To this day, some Claflin graduates Sid has mentored continue to call or visit him in New York, talk to him about their careers, ask his advice on professional or personal questions, and thank him for supporting, encouraging, and mentoring them.

* "Biography," Paul Robeson Foundation. www. paulrobesonfoundation.org/biography.html.

no fundraising and that we would help all charities." The program was an immediate success. Sid arranged for former commissioners of the IRS, assistant Treasury secretaries for tax policy, the leading surrogate judges, and the top names in the legal and accounting professions to speak at the conference. Each year, hundreds of people turn out for this program, which is held at the most prestigious hotels in New York. In September 2012, the UJA-Federation will hold the 43rd Annual Sidney Kess New York Estate, Tax & Financial Planning Conference. The conference has become a model for other charities whose representatives participate in the program. Sid said other charities, including the Catholic Diocese of New York, often ask him to guide them in conducting a similar program.

Campbell University

For 25 years, Sid visited Campbell University in Buies Creek, North Carolina every year. Founded as Buies Creek Academy in1887 by James Archibald Campbell, a preacher, the school offers liberal arts, education, religion, and other academic programs. His visits began as the result of a monetary donation given to the school to hold programs for the public as well as students. The school had previously held some public programs, but the turnouts were small. The school decided to invite Sid to hold a one-day program for CPAs and others in the community about tax and other issues of interest to them. Not surprisingly, Sid was a big draw.

On his visits, Sid talks to students, in individual meetings or in groups, about careers, what directions to take, and life in general. Some of the top students often are invited to visit the nearby estate of a famous author with Sid. Sid will spend an afternoon and evening guiding them on their careers. "Many of the students are the first in their families to attend college. One thing I tried to impress upon them was to thank their parents and others who were making sacrifices to make their education possible. It's a small thing, but sometimes we forget to thank those who have helped us along the way."

Baruch College

Sid organized and ran an estate planning conference at Baruch College for a number of years. Today, the program is known as the Zicklin Tax Seminar Series and is offered in cooperation with Sid.

Fordham University

Sid has talked about careers to students at Fordham University, using as an example Cecil Nazareth. With Sid's advice and encouragement, Nazareth became a recognized leader in IFRS, and he is now a partner with IFRS Partners, a New York firm that provides education, training, and consulting in IFRS. (For more, see Cecil Nazareth's account on p. 31–32).

Sid

2

Build and Maintain Core Knowledge and Expertise

Early in his career, as a result of his talent for analyzing and interpreting tax law, Sid became a foremost tax expert. He spent hours studying proposed or newly enacted changes in tax laws and regulations. He talked with other tax practitioners and people in government about tax issues. Sid stayed current on tax questions of interest to fellow practitioners and clients.

In addition to building a deep base of knowledge, Sid was able to maintain expertise already gained, while branching off into new areas.

This hard work paid off with his becoming a national director of taxes for one of the largest public accounting firms in the United States and a nationally known continuing professional education (CPE) lecturer.

As a nationally renowned tax expert, Sid has an extraordinary ability to delve into the tax code, plumb its depths, study its sometimes confusing language, and explain it in plain English. "The unique aspect of Sid's speaking and writing is that he always starts with the big picture, captures the key concepts, and reduces them to understandable terms," said Martin Shenkman, CPA, PFS, JD, an estate planner in Paramus, NJ. "Sid's diligence in simplifying the technical is a model for us all." (Shenkman comments further on p. 102)

Sid's Career Highlights

Sid is both a CPA and a lawyer, having earned a bachelor's degree in accounting from New York's Baruch College, a law degree from Harvard University School of Law, and a master of laws degree in taxation from New York University.

Education		
Baruch College	BBA	1948
Harvard University School of Law	JD	1952
New York University Graduate School of Law	LLM	1955

During his career in public accounting, Sid was a director of tax training, national director of taxes, and a national tax partner, and he is now of counsel to a New York law firm.

Public Accounting		
Firm	Title	Years employed
Lybrand Ross & Montgomery	Director of Tax Training	1952–1969
Main Lafrentz & Co.	National Director of Taxes	1969–1987
Main Hurdman	National Director of Taxes	1969–1987
KMG Main Hurdman	National Director of Taxes	1969–1987
KPMG Peat Marwick	National Tax Partner	1987–1988
Law		
Kostelanetz & Fink New York	Of Counsel	2010–present

Since the 1960s, Sid has lectured to more than 750,000 practitioners on tax, financial, and estate planning. As one of the foremost teachers in CPE, he has led hundreds of conferences on tax, financial, and estate planning hosted by the AICPA as well as other entities. He has written and edited many articles, reports, courses, study aids, and books and created a number of video and audio presentations on income tax and financial and estate planning for the AICPA and CCH, a Wolters Kluwer business. For more than 40 years, Sid has edited the *Tax Tips* column for the *New York Law Journal* and, for just as long, he has chaired the New York Estate, Tax & Financial Planning Conference, sponsored by the UJA-Federation of New York. He is frequently quoted in the *Wall Street Journal*, the *New York Times*, and other publications.

"Sid is an original thinker in his approach to both problems and their solutions, amply connecting the [tax] rules to their application," said Gary S. Lesser, an independent benefits consultant, author, and software developer.[1] "And he's been doing it for so long, you would think he wrote the rules himself!"

"Sid is, without question, the all-time number one developer, writer, and presenter in the world of CPE for CPAs, not only for the AICPA but the accounting profession as a whole," said L. Paden Neeley, PhD, CPA, retired. Mr. Needly is a former VP of the AICPA.

CPE Lecturer		
Workshop/Conference	**Sponsor**	**Year(s)**
New York State Society of CPAs Tax Workshop	New York State Society of CPAs	1964–2004
AICPA Individual and Corporate Tax Workshops	AICPA	1965–2004
Tax & Financial Planning Conferences and Workshops	AICPA	1987–2012
Sidney Kess New York Estate, Tax & Financial Planning Conference	UJA-Federation of New York	1969–present
Ultimate Estate, Retirement & Financial Planning National Conference	PESI	2000–2010
Tax Update Conference	Baruch College	8 Years
Tax Conference for Public and Students	Campbell University	1980–2005

Over time, CPAs and other professionals in similar fields have turned to Sid not only for tax advice but also for guidance on how they can develop the knowledge and expertise to start and grow businesses, develop expertise in areas such as financial planning or International Financial Reporting Standards, and establish their reputations as CPE firms, leading tax practitioners, experts in different fields, and prominent lecturers.

---

1   Gary S. Lesser is a contributing author and technical editor of the *CPA's Guide to Retirement Plans for Small Businesses* and *The Adviser's Guide to Health Savings Accounts*, published by the AICPA, as well as the publisher of *Basic Accounting Simplified*.

Getting Started in Financial Planning Services

For CPAs, the marketing of financial planning services begins with their existing clients.

Helping CPAs Succeed in Financial Planning

Andrea Millar, CPA/PFS, leads the AICPA Personal Financial Division:

I had the pleasure of meeting Sid on a panel at the AICPA's Advanced Tax Strategies for High-Income Individuals conference in May, 2007. The purpose of the panel was to make sure attendees were aware of the many resources available to them via AICPA to assist them in being successful in practice, one of Sid's many missions to help CPA practitioners.

Sid and I bonded right away since he was the national director of taxes at KMG Main Hurdman and a tax partner at KPMG Peat Marwick, and I had spent a good amount of my career as a CPA financial planner at KPMG LLP.

From the very moment Sid understood my role and mission to help CPAs be successful in financial planning, he never missed a beat in always having his thinking cap on to push the cause forward. Below are a few of the takeaways from this experience with Sid:

- *Relationships, relationships, relationships.* Sid and I could have been on this 30-minute panel and easily never spoken again. But instead, he took the initiative to understand my mission (helping CPAs to be successful in financial planning) and how it related to his passion (helping *everyone* be successful, that is, consumers, CPAs, attorneys, educators, for-profit and non-

About 60 percent of individual taxpayers pay preparers to do their returns.[2] CPAs that prepare returns could use this opportunity to suggest tax and other financial planning services to clients. "Use the 1040 as a road map for financial planning," Sid advised. CPAs can use the checklist prepared by the AICPA's Personal Financial Planning section for reviewing tax returns and go over the list with clients to find opportunities for income deferral, plan for the care of elderly parents, or create a succession plan for a business.[3] If CPAs begin preparing returns for new clients, they can take the same approach in looking for financial planning opportunities.

Using a Checklist

Part of the challenge for CPAs going into financial planning services is to convince existing or prospective clients that they need such services in the first place. Sid and Steven G. Siegel, JD, LLM, president of The Siegel Group, have written a detailed checklist, with added contributions from CPAs, attorneys, and other professionals, listing the reasons clients should seek financial planning assistance immediately.[4] As Sid noted in

---

2   "Introduction: The Most Serious Problems Encountered by Taxpayers," National Taxpayers Advocate, Internal Revenue Service, 2010, www.irs.gov/pub/irs-utl/2010arcmsp1_taxreform.pdf.

3   "Analysis of a Tax Return for Personal Financial Planning," AICPA Personal Financial Planning Division. www.aicpa.org/interestareas/personalfinancialplanning/resources/taxplanning/downloadabledocuments/analysisofataxreturnforpfp.pdf.

4   "101 (And More) Reasons Why Clients Should Seek Financial Planning Assistance Now," Prepared by Sidney Kess, Esq., CPA and Steven G. Siegel, JD, LLM, www.aicpa.

a prelude to the list, "clients do not have to be especially wealthy or old or ill to need planning." In fact, the best time to start planning is when clients are young, healthy, and just starting their adult lives.

The purpose of this checklist is to make clients, as well as planners, aware of the many issues and questions to address in financial planning, such as the client's asset and liability position; future plans; whether to rebalance an investment portfolio; education planning, including college savings vehicles; present or future social security benefits; and beneficiary designation issues.

Promoting Awareness

The AICPA and other organizations have been promoting public awareness of the need for financial planning. Sid was honorary co-chair of National Estate Planning Awareness Week 2011, which dedicates the third week of October to promoting estate planning. It is a project of the National Association of Estate Planners and Councils and the NAEPC Foundation.[5]

Developing Knowledge

Another challenge for CPAs going into financial planning services is developing the knowledge, experience, and resources to provide such services

profit organizations, and so forth) and brought the two together. This led to a wonderful and fulfilling relationship that has produced tremendous results and will only grow in the future.

- *Always stay positive and keep the big picture at the forefront.* Sid always finds the opportunities and positives in every situation and never loses sight of the end goal. When Sid learned that many CPAs have a misperception that financial planning is managing money and/or selling products, he developed many ideas to overcome this obstacle that have led CPAs to get the help they need in advising individuals in estate, retirement, tax, investments, and insurance and in growing the number of CPAs providing this service to their clients.

- *What goes around comes around.* Sid has a huge following of people who respect, adore, and admire him and would do anything for him. He is the master of building relationships and then putting people and organizations together in win-win situations that ultimately help the end users: the CPA practitioners. He'll identify the most knowledgeable and skilled experts in the country and make sure they are plugged in with all of the right organizations. This not only serves the success of the experts and the organizations but also ensures that the end users are getting the best of the best to be successful in practice.

The bottom line is that Sid Kess is a one-of-a-kind human being with a heart of gold. When he walks in a room, it is as if a beam of light is lit from within. I am truly honored to have Sid Kess in my life.

and being able to compete with non-CPA financial planners, banks, and others who offer similar services. Some CPAs may already be providing some

---

org/interestareas/personalfinancialplanning/cpeandevents/downloadabledocuments/financialestateplanningchecklist.pdf.

5   "National Estate Planning Awareness Week and Estate Planning Day Materials," National Association of Estate Planners and Councils. www.naepc.org/estate_planning_week.web

degree of financial planning for clients by virtue of doing tax preparation and tax planning, or they may be providing some financial planning advice to clients who are small business owners,[6] but they may want to make more of a commitment to financial planning.

In that event, important considerations are what types of clients they want to serve (for example, wealthy individuals, high salary professionals, middle income teachers, and so forth), and what services they want to offer (for example, particular services such as estate planning or a broader range of services). Services may be offered as a supplement to a firm's core audit or tax services, as a separate firm service, or through a separate entity created by the firm.[7]

Because financial planning services require accounting, legal, investment advisory, and other skills that usually are beyond the capabilities of a single firm, practitioners must recognize the value of building relationships and networks with other practitioners and firms. Such connections can provide access to specialized expertise that best serves the interests of clients.[8] Another option for a firm is to join one of the growing numbers of associations of accounting firms that operate globally.[9] One of the key purposes of these associations is to meet client demand for services, expertise, and resources anywhere in the world.[10]

Whatever direction they take, CPAs may want to advance their knowledge by earning a bachelor's or master's degree in financial planning or a related subject, taking continuing education courses, or obtaining certification through programs offered by the AICPA and various other organizations. Sid recommends that CPAs obtain certification under the AICPA's Personal Financial Specialist (PFS) program.[11]

---

6   Roger Russell, "Tax To Financial Planning: A Natural Progression," *Accounting Today*, November 1, 2011,www.accountingtoday.com/ato_issues/25_11/tax-to-financial-planning-a-natural-progression-60563-1.html.

7   "Roadmap to Developing and Managing a CPA Personal Financial Planning Practice," AICPA Personal Financial Planning Section, www.aicpa.org/interestareas/personalfinancialplanning/resources/pfppracticemanagement/pfppracticeguides/downloadabledocuments/10781-378_booklet-final.pdf.

8   Sid Kess, CPA, JD, and Steven Siegel, JD, LLM, "The Financial and Estate Planner: Why practitioners need to recognize the need for teamwork to build mutually beneficial relationships with other practitioners or informal networks," *Wealth Management Insider*, May 19, 2011, www.cpa2biz.com/Content/media/PRODUCER_CONTENT/Newsletters/Articles_2011/Wealth/Estate_Planner.jsp.

9   "2011 Annual Directory of CPA Firm Associations and Networks," CCH. www.integra-international.net/files/files/2010_%20Annual_CCH_Directory_of_CPA_Firms_and_Associations.pdf.

10   "This Isn't Your Father's Association' International Business Drives Membership," *Public Accounting Report*, February 15, 2011, Vol. 35, Issue 3.

11   "Overview of the Personal Financial Specialist Program," AICPA, www.aicpa.org/InterestAreas/PersonalFinancialPlanning/Membership/Pages/OverviewofthePersonalFinancialSpecialist(PFS)Credential.aspx.

Some Personal Thoughts about Sidney Kess, CPA

Written by Calvin R. Swinson, CPA

I met Sidney Kess while employed by Lybrand, Ross Bros. and Montgomery, CPAs, now PriceWaterhouseCoopers. As one of two black professional employees at the time, life was very interesting, to say the least. Taking and passing the CPA examination was mandatory, if one wanted to have any chance of success. Shortly after joining the firm in July 1963, I met Mr. Kess. Mr. Kess immediately began to stress the need for me to do well and pass the CPA examination.

Often, he would talk to me about the importance of education and how my having gone to both undergraduate and graduate school should have prepared me well for passing the examination and doing well at the firm. Having been away from accounting for a few years due to military service and working for the federal government, I decided to take his coaching course. The course was very popular and many candidates in the firm and elsewhere took it to bone-up on the CPA examination.

After taking his course, I was successful in passing the examination in September 1966. I became one of the first African-Americans employed by one of the then "Big Eight" firms to pass the examination.

Shortly after passing the examination, I left public accounting and entered private accounting before returning to public accounting a few years later.

Mr. Kess's counseling, motivation, and inspiration, as well as continuous reminders to me of the need to stay current in my profession, have served me well in life. Mr. Kess preaches the importance of education and the benefits of it. He is a unique professional and a true believer in helping the underdog.

Educating Practitioners

Sid was among the first professionals to recognize the increasing demand for financial planning services and to suggest strategies for CPAs to capture a share of this growing market. Because many CPAs were unfamiliar with this market, they first had to learn about it. "In the 1980s, Sid worked with the New York State Society of CPAs to educate them," said Walter M. Primoff, CPA/PFS. Primoff is director of the Professional Advisory Group, Altfest Personal Wealth Management, and past deputy executive director of the New York State Society. Primoff joined the New York Society in the mid-1980s, when the profession was undergoing transformative regulatory and competitive changes, a process that continues to this day. "Sid foresaw the impact of these changes on CPAs," Primoff said.

Sid Kess: A True Teacher

Bryan C. Skarlatos

My first introduction to Sid Kess was the smiling photograph of him printed in the pages of the *New York Law Journal* where Sid writes a regular column on *Tax Tips*. It seems to me that I have been reading about Sid ever since I became a lawyer some 25 years ago. I have learned now that Sid has been writing that Tax Tips column since I was in elementary school. We won't mention how long ago that was. Suffice it to say that Sid has been a fountain of knowledge and experience in the New York tax community for a long time.

Sid's reputation was one of the reasons why I was thrilled to meet him at a meeting of the Advisory Board of the New York University (NYU) Graduate Tax Institute. On the NYU Advisory Board, I got to see Sid in action. He is an idea man who knows how to work with people and address problems in a practical, solution-oriented way. Pulling from his years of experience teaching tax across the country and producing the highest quality, most successful tax programs, Sid is able to shoot out suggestion after suggestion on how to improve any conference or organization.

Over the years, I have gotten to know Sid very well, and I am proud to count him as a friend as well as a professional colleague. I was overjoyed and honored when he became Of Counsel at my firm, Kostelanetz & Fink, LLP in New York City. Ever since joining the firm, Sid has continued to impart his wisdom to senior and junior lawyers alike. He is constantly exhorting all of us to become better attorneys, to become more active in bar association activities, and to publish and lecture as much as our busy schedules will permit. And he leads by example. He continues to publish and speak with a frequency that would be difficult for two people half his age. Needless to say, Sid has become an invaluable part of Kostelanetz & Fink, LLP.

My impression of Sid can be best summarized by a short anecdote. I was speaking with Sid in the hallway of one of the innumerable tax conferences that he produces and hosts. A young accountant came striding up to Sid with his hand outstretched and said, "Mr. Kess, I just wanted to shake the hand of the man who taught tax to my grandfather and my father." Sid smiled broadly and graciously replied that he was honored to be involved in the education of three generations of tax practitioners. How many teachers can say that?

Sid is an inspiration to us all and an example of how important it is to constantly share our knowledge and experience to help others. I know he taught me a lot. Thank you, Sid.

Assisting Firms

In addition to educating CPAs on financial planning, Sid has worked with CPA firms on expanding into the field.

Jonathan Gassman is a third generation member of Gassman and Golodny, a New York-based tax and financial planning boutique. His grandfather, who is the firm's founder, Gassman, and his father have all attended Sid's Individual Income Tax Workshops and Corporate Tax Workshops over the years.

Sid helped the firm diversify into the financial planning field. "With our analytic skills, our inquisitive nature, and the degree of skepticism that we bring to the table, it was a natural and logical step for us," Gassman said. "As the trusted advisor to the client, who is best to serve as the client's personal CFO?" he noted. "'There is no one better to provide these services than the CPA,' Sid would tell me."

Developing Expertise in Financial Planning Services

Suppose, for example, your firm is considering whether or not to expand into financial planning services. The following is Sid's perspective on this market:

Today, the opportunities for CPAs to provide financial planning services continue to grow. Part of the reason for this is due to the broad definition of *financial planning*: managing one's finances to achieve life goals, such as attending college, raising a family, starting a business, retiring, or contributing to charity. Financial planning services include the following:

- *Personal financial planning*, such as assisting clients to establish financial goals, plan budgets, develop strategies for money management, establish savings and retirement plans, and evaluate investment opportunities

- *Income tax planning*, including identifying opportunities to minimize taxes, identifying risks that could result in adverse tax consequences, analyzing the tax consequences of financial decisions, and tax structuring of investments

- *Investment planning*, including reviewing clients' investment preferences and risk tolerance to help them develop appropriate investment strategies, discussing available investment options with clients, and monitoring the performance of invested assets

- *Insurance planning*, such as analyzing client exposure to risks and recommending methods for managing risk and advising clients on various types and uses of life insurance

- *Retirement planning*, including helping clients develop or refine retirement planning goals and determining cash requirements to realize those goals

- *Estate planning*, including estimating liabilities for federal estate tax, state death taxes, and other obligations; reviewing tax and probate considerations for various forms of property ownership; and developing strategies for minimizing estate and death taxes.

The Expert Advantage

"In the early stages of my career, professionals were generalists—everyone knew a little of everything," Sid noted. "Now, more and more are experts."

More CPAs are becoming experts: someone with the education, experience, and comprehensive knowledge to be recognized as an authority on a subject. The reasons for becoming an expert vary:

- *The explosion of knowledge.* Knowledge generally, and in specialized areas such as taxes, pensions, and estate planning, is growing at an exponential rate, creating more demand for experts.

- *Clients require expertise.* A client may need not only a CPA, but also a forensic accountant, to develop a computer system to protect against fraud, investigate internal fraud, or to provide other forensic services. Another client may need a tax practitioner with expertise in state and local taxes or international taxes. Yet another may want an expert in bankruptcy reorganization.

- *CPA firms need experts.* Public accounting firms may need to recruit or develop experts to meet client demand, serve niche markets, and develop new business.

- *The scope of expertise is expanding.* Clients and firms require CPAs who not only are experts in functions, such as pensions or forensic accounting, but also in industries, such as financial services, real estate, health care, or computer technology.

- *New knowledge and ideas are creating needs for new expertise.* An example is the emerging field of integrated reporting, which takes a holistic view of a company or other organization.[12] It integrates into a single report all of a company's reports that previously have been published separately, such as its annual reports, reports on the sustainability of a firm's business practices, or reports on corporate social responsibility. It provides a broad picture of the environmental, social, political, financial, and other forces impacting a company and has wide applications, such as in managing risk.

Sid has the following suggestions for CPAs who want to become experts. They can be young professionals just starting their careers or experienced professionals who want to acquire expertise, make a career change, or reinvent themselves as professionals:

---

12   Jonathan Shaw, "A Revolution in Corporate Reporting," *Harvard Magazine*, March-April 2011, http://harvardmagazine.com/2011/03/revolution-in-corporate-reporting.

> *"You have as much of an opportunity to become an expert as everyone else." — Sid*

- *Everyone starts at the same line in learning.* "You have as much of an opportunity to become an expert as everyone else," Sid observed. The best opportunities are in relatively new fields. A prime example is the new health care law, the Patient Protection and Affordable Care Act. "You can jump into it, learn about it, and develop expertise," Sid noted. But opportunities can also be found in developing expertise in established specialties. For example, in an economic downturn, more companies and businesses may need expertise in bankruptcy reorganizations.

- *Begin as a generalist.* "Before you begin to specialize, get experience across your organization," Sid advises. Work in audit, tax, or other core areas. Get to know people in your organization by finding out who they are and what they do.

- *Consider a specialization path.* What interests you? Start by doing research. Talk to experts inside and outside your organization. Research the websites of CPA firms and other companies that offer expert services. Check out the sites of professional societies and trade organizations whose members are experts in a particular field. Read trade journals. Once you decide on a specialty, you can narrow your focus. Do online research, take online classes, take courses at your local college, and go to conferences sponsored by professional societies and trade organizations. Read, study, and learn. Talk to experts about how they became experts. Obtain credentials in your area of expertise. In addition to the Personal Financial Specialist certification, the AICPA has credential programs in financial forensics, business valuation, and information technology. Other organizations offer credential programs, for example, the Association of Certified Fraud Examiners issues a Certified Fraud Examiner certificate.

- *Look for opportunities to develop expertise.* These opportunities include learning about new laws; changes to existing tax or other laws; new or revised rules and regulations; and new accounting rules or changes to existing rules, such as proposed lease accounting standards, trends in the economy, such as the growth of international trade, or in industries, such as the growth of green standards and practices in construction.

- *Think globally.* You may find opportunities to become an expert in the international arena. An example follows:

  — In January, 2012, a joint venture of the AICPA and the London-based Chartered Institute of Management Accountants (CIMA) launched a new designation, the Chartered Global Management Accountant (CGMA). The CGMA is intended to be the leading global designation for business. Beginning in the first quarter of 2012, AICPA voting members will be automatically eligible for the credential upon verifying three years of qualifying experience.[13]

- *Get known.* Establish your authority as an expert by writing articles, participating in panels, and speaking to groups. Observe other experts speaking at conferences, workshops, and other venues. Observe how they present information in a manner that captures the audience's interest. "Develop your own personal style as an expert," Sid advises. "Show that you have the breadth and depth of knowledge and the communication skills expected of an expert. Act like an expert, and you'll be accepted as an expert."

Sid Helps Others Become Experts

With Sid's guidance and support, Joseph D. Mach, currently an international examiner with the IRS, became an expert on the Employee Retirement Income Security Act of 1974 and, later in his career, on international taxation.

In 1974, when I was 29 years old, Sid was the head of taxation at Main Hurdman. He asked me if I was interested in becoming an expert on a new pension law that was working its way through Congress. I had never worked in the benefits and pension area, but I agreed.

I was able to hit the ground running as an "instant expert" (Sid's term for me) when the legislation, now known as ERISA, was signed on Labor Day, 1974. (ERISA, or the Employee Retirement Income Security Act, is a federal law that sets minimum standards for pension plans in private industry.[14])

Late in September, 1974, the firm had a national tax meeting. Sid wanted me to speak on the new ERISA law, but there were objections within the firm to having such a junior person, five years out of law school, as a speaker.

An outside firm partner was supposed to talk, but mysteriously never showed up. At breakfast, less than 45 minutes before the speaker was supposed to talk, Sid told me that I would speak. Somehow, I gave a talk that was well received.

---

13 "American Institute of Certified Public Accountants and Chartered Institute of Management Accountants Agree to Offer New CGMA Designation," AICPA/ CIMA press release, May 23, 2011, www.aicpa.org/press/pressreleases/2011/pages/ aicpaandcimaagreetonewcgmadesignation.aspx.

14 United States Department of Labor, "The Employee Retirement Security Income Act (ERISA)," www.dol.gov/compliance/laws/comp-erisa.htm.

I spent the rest of my time at Main Lafrentz/Main Hurdman giving speeches around the country on ERISA and LIFO, another area in which Sid encouraged me. Sid also got me a column on ERISA and benefits in The Practical Accountant Magazine, which I wrote from 1976–1988.

I served as the National Director of ERISA and Employee Benefits taxation for more than six years, helping clients of the firm comply with the new law.

At Main Lafrentz, Sid and another partner, Dick Stone, were friendly, helpful, supportive, and demanding in the best sense. They were the best bosses I ever had, and I still consider both of them as good friends whom I would invite, and have invited, to family celebrations.

I kept in touch with Sid even after I left Main Hurdman to go into industry. Later, when I was back in public accounting as a senior manager and, later, partner, in both benefits and international taxation at BDO Seidman, he helped me obtain a position as an adjunct tax professor at Fordham graduate business school and encouraged me to resume my public speaking.

About five years ago, I attended a symposium at Baruch College in honor of Sid. He had me stand up, and he spoke of my accomplishments—some that I remembered and others that I had forgotten. By the end of the evening, I had a part-time job teaching at Baruch.

Three years ago, my job in industry was eliminated, and I figured that my career was over. Sid disagreed and encouraged me to apply to the IRS for an international examiner position. With Sid as a reference, I got the job."

I owe much of my career to Sid Kess—friend, mentor, reference, job coach. Whenever I need him, Sid is there. As the Yiddish expression goes, "may he live to 120, and may my face be the last one he sees."

Developing expertise in International Financial Reporting Standards

Cecil Nazareth, CPA, is managing partner of IFRS Partners in New York, a firm that provides consulting and educational services on International Financial Reporting Standards (IFRS).

I met Sid 20 years ago when I took his income tax update course. Then, five years ago, I got reacquainted with Sid when I worked at the AICPA, and we collaborated on some joint projects. I learned a lot from him and asked him to be my mentor. He agreed and has been my mentor ever since.

When Sid learned that I was a Chartered Accountant and a CPA, he asked me to pursue the new growth field of IFRS. He helped me reinvent myself at a pivotal point in my professional career.

Sid told me that in a new field everyone is at the same starting point. If you focus on the growth area, you could be one of its leading experts, a thought leader, and compete with professionals who have been in the field for 25 years.

(continued on pg. 32)

(continued from pg. 31)

I took his advice four years ago. I have since delivered hundreds of sessions on IFRS for CCH, the AICPA, various stock exchanges all around the world, and some large U.S. CPA firms. I have also developed my own IFRS Web series. I am currently on the faculty of Fordham University (New York) teaching IFRS and global financial analysis at the graduate and undergraduate level.

Sid continues to inspire me and coach me. He encourages me to pursue knowledge and growth in my personal and professional life. I am thankful and grateful for all that he has done for me. I enjoy what I do and continue to be a teacher and a student and to give back with honor and integrity.

From public accounting to expert in tax incentives for energy efficient real estate

Karen J. Koch is a CPA in Shelbyville, Kentucky.

After many years in public accounting, I decided to step out into the consulting world. I focus on providing engineering and tax expertise to commercial real estate owners in the use of tax and energy incentives.

Attending a New York tax conference in 2008, I was introduced to Sid, who listened as I shared my passion to become a resource to CPA firms by delivering services they usually don't provide. Sid connected me with leaders in our profession and in the AICPA, and I was invited to participate in the AICPA's Trusted Advisor program, an online tool for CPAs to connect with resources to support their practices. As part of the program, I was to do a video with Sid on the subject of cost segregation.

The day for taping the video arrived, and, filled with excitement and anxiety, I took a morning flight from Louisville to New York. I wondered if I would really be able to meet Sid's expectations. At that time, I knew him as a pillar of the profession but not on a personal level. I arrived in New York, went to the recording studio, and the taping began, with Sid and I talking about cost segregation. His gentle smile of affirmation helped me to slip into a comfortable place and gain confidence—a great gift he gave me for many future public speaking opportunities.

As soon as we finished the taping, Sid took me to a New York tax conference, where he introduced me as a "trusted advisor" and gave me the opportunity to share my story. Thus began the branding process that has led to my success.

Since then, because Sid cared enough to make a difference in my life, I have built a career in assisting CPAs to introduce innovative sustainability planning strategies to their service lines and, in the process, add value to their services. My career has rewarded me with the joys of helping others and making many new friends, as well as the challenge of continuing to learn and give back each day.

Sid is most deserving of honor and recognition for his innumerable contributions to the CPA profession and to us as individual CPAs. To follow his example means we never stop learning and we never stop giving back.

> *"To follow his example means we never stop learning and we never stop giving back."*

Managing a Practice

Throughout his career, Sid has provided advice to individual CPAs, firms, and tax practitioners on how they can start and manage a practice, market their services, recruit talented employees, win and keep clients, and grow their businesses.

Sid wrote a book, *Managing a Profitable Tax Practice: Text, Forms and Procedures*, that was published in 1972 by Warren, Gorham & Lamont. From the book, the following are some of Sid's suggestions for business development:

- *Market your ideas.* Many of the CPA firms in the United States are small firms (see table 2.1), and they face a particular challenge in competing with larger firms with more people and resources. But in the marketplace for ideas, all firms are on a level playing field. Any CPA or firm can suggest ideas for helping clients to reduce taxes, plan for retirement, anticipate the effects of proposed changes in tax laws or rulings, or otherwise benefit from a CPA's advice.

Table 2.1 U.S. CPA Firms by Employment Size (2007)

Size of Firm	Number of Firms
0–4 employees	36,394
5–9 employees	10,152
10–19 employees	4,442
20–99 employees	2,178
100–499 employees	245
500+	75
TOTAL	53,486

(Source: U.S. Census Bureau: Statistics of U.S. Businesses, 2009, Office of Certified Public Accountants—by Employment Size of Enterprise, www.census.gov/econ/susb/)

Firms should take the initiative to present ideas to clients and stay in communication with them, for example, by emailing links to articles and

Benefits of Multiple Degrees

Sid has a bachelor's degree in accounting, a law degree, and a master of laws in taxation. These multiple degrees have given him a broader and deeper knowledge of these fields. For example, he said an undergraduate accounting course might include a general textbook on tax, but it would not examine estate planning or pensions in much detail. By contrast, a master's program in taxation would include courses in which estate planning or pensions would be examined in depth. Likewise, an accounting graduate who enrolled in law school would study bankruptcy reorganization, estate planning practice and procedure, securities law, and other subjects not covered in an accounting curriculum. If an accounting graduate studies for an MBA, the curriculum could include investment finance, doing business internationally, and other new subjects. "This gives you more confidence if you are working with professionals in different disciplines or sitting with them in a meeting," Sid said. Studying for a law degree enables accounting graduates to refine their critical thinking and problem-solving skills. "Legal training helps you to prepare for any situation you encounter in the professional world. You learn to analyze the facts, examine the issues, and come up with a conclusion based on the facts. You gain confidence, and you are not afraid to deal with any problem."

reports in newspapers or magazines that may be of interest to clients. They should continue to offer ideas on a consistent basis. Although not every idea will resonate with a client, firms should have a follow-up procedure to capitalize on those that are relevant and applicable. Clients look to firms for ideas and suggestions on how they can monetize them.

As an example of the power of ideas, Sid recalls that at age 75, Max Rolnick merged his accounting firm, Leslie Banks & Company, with Coopers & Lybrand. Sid asked Rolnick how his firm had built up such great clientele that it was an attractive merger partner for Coopers. Rolnick said he always went into client meetings with 10 or 15 ideas about ways his firm could help the client and, if even one idea clicked, clients were ecstatic.

Conversely, a paucity of ideas can result in a loss of business. Sid recalled that when he was national tax director of KPMG Main Hurdman, he flew to one of the firm's local offices to learn why it had lost a client. "The client said it never came up with any ideas," he said.

• *Two Words: Ideas and Client.* Jim Avedisian, a CPA and estate planning attorney based in Los Altos, California, said, "If there were only two words to make me think of Sid, they would be *ideas* and *client.*"

"I first met Sid in 1984 when I spoke at a CCH conference in Washington, D.C., with Sid serving as the chairman of the conference. It was one of the first national conferences at which I spoke. Because of Sid's drawing power, the conference was oversold, and I had to give my talk twice, in two different rooms.

With that start, we developed a friendship that included my speaking at his AICPA Tax Strategies for the High-Income Individual conference for 18 years and serving on his steering committee for 6 years.

What I learned from Sid is that if the CPA focuses on the client and presents ideas, the rest is easy. I still practice that way."

> *"...if the CPA focuses on the client and presents ideas, the rest is easy."*

• *Capitalize on new developments.* Firms should keep clients informed of developments in Congress, the capital markets, and the business world that might affect their businesses and tell them promptly of proposed tax laws or rules, proposed changes to existing laws, and how they might capitalize on the opportunities or minimize the risks that would result from such changes. For example, there is much uncertainty about what actions Congress might take to further reduce the deficit. One question is whether Congress might reduce the $5 million-per-individual estate tax exemption to $1 million and increase the top estate tax rate to 55 percent from the current 35 percent. To hedge against that risk, clients might consider making gifts right away.

Another example is the Affordable Care Act. Signed into law in 2010, it puts into place comprehensive health insurance reforms that roll out over four years and beyond, with most changes taking place by 2014—that is, unless Congress or the courts intervene. Firms should study the law and meet with clients to discuss its effects, including the effects on clients' taxes, and discuss how clients can respond.

Firms also need to stay abreast of changes in tax regulations and alert clients. For example, in September 2011, the IRS announced that it was offering a break to employers who own up to misclassifying employees as independent contractors. Employers accepted into a new IRS program must reclassify workers as employees and pay a small percentage of the wages paid to the workers for the past year. No interest or penalties would be due. Firms could meet with clients who might be affected by the IRS offer and discuss how to respond.

As another example, in 2010, the IRS revised its *Cash Intensive Businesses Audit Technique Guide* for cash businesses. Since then, it has been updated periodically, most recently in November 2011. If you have clients in cash intensive businesses, such as beauty shops, car washes, or convenience stores, you may point out what the IRS is looking for regarding the cash business.

Stay in front of clients throughout the year. Each month, focus on a different service area, such as cost segregation, retirement plans, or fringe benefits. Send them an e-mail or newsletter that discusses that month's topic. If a communication sparks a client's interest, schedule a meeting to discuss it further.

• *Don't overlook state legislation.* Be sure to track proposed state legislation or changes to existing state laws that could affect your clients. For example, New York State's 2011 law allowing same-sex marriages raises questions of health benefit taxes and estate taxes, filings of state and federal taxes, and other questions for same-sex couples.

• *Schedule year-end tax meetings.* Send a year-end tax planning letter to your clients. You can create the letter in-house or order one from a publishing house. Follow up your letter by scheduling year-end tax meetings with clients to review plans for the preparation of returns, estimate tax payments, and plan strategies, including how to address tax issues, capitalize on tax incentives, and minimize tax obligations. If you acquire a new client, see if you can pick up errors that were made in prior year returns to get possible refunds. You can use checklists available from the AICPA to assist with tax reviews and planning.

• *Stay focused on developing new business.* Start with your existing clients. Ask them to refer business to you, and be sure to reciprocate if they help you. Send them a gift, and send business their way if you can.

Banks are another source for referrals. Some may agree to have you speak to their clients about a tax issue or other topic.

Cultivate attorneys as clients by sending the IRS audit guide to attorney friends. Develop special knowledge and skills, for example, in state and local taxes or by forming a corporation, and impress attorneys with your expertise.

Cultivate close relationships with insurance and investment specialists. Like attorneys, they may refer business, and opportunities may exist to collaborate with them in marketing to clients.

Contact prospective clients to schedule a meeting with them along with a benefits consultant. You might review retirement plans for executives and employees.

Consider hiring a specialist in marketing accounting services.

• *Recommend an expert when necessary.* If a client has a need that is beyond your firm's expertise or research capability, don't feel insecure about recommending a specialist. The client will appreciate that you are being attentive to their needs.

- *Invest in technology and training.* Make the investment in technology that will enable your firm to provide the best service and attract talented people. Provide training in-house or pay for training programs offered by service providers.

- *Always be responsive to clients.* If your client leaves a voicemail or e-mail message asking you to contact them, get back to them immediately. "This is so important," Sid noted. "Everyone likes a prompt response. But some people never get back to you."

- *Learn to manage change.* To develop and grow their businesses, CPAs must learn to manage change. Sid has long worked with firms on change management. Some years ago, he assisted the previously mentioned (page 26–27) Gassman and Golodny firm with the creation of a tax binder for all its employees, giving them quick access to charts, tables, and facts while working in the field with clients. Then the computer age dawned, and the firm had to adapt. "It was because of Sid that our firm transitioned from preparing tax returns with input sheets to buying our first personal computer and in-house tax preparation software," Jonathan Gassman said.

Gassman said Sid's help didn't stop there:

— Sid's connections to people at the IRS helped the firm to close many tax audits, as well as find the answers to unresolved tax questions.

— Sid always was ready to share practice management tips, for example, suggesting "simple single doable things" (SSDTs) that the firm could quickly implement and see tangible results.

— "Sid's given us lots of great marketing ideas that have helped us penetrate markets we might not have been able to penetrate without his guidance." Sid had ideas for newsletters, webinars, client

Always Be Responsive

By advising CPAs to always be responsive to their clients, Sid practices what he preaches in his relationships—with everyone. "During the past 20 plus years, I have participated as an instructor in many of his workshops and conferences," said Seymour Goldberg, senior partner of Goldberg & Goldberg P.C., a Woodbury, NY law firm. "He is truly a class act and, at any time that I need advice, he is always there." Cecilia Anthony, Sid's former personal assistant, who worked at the AICPA for 12 years, said, "He is totally dedicated to the AICPA and the CPA profession and continues to volunteer ideas to make the AICPA more valuable to its members. He has made himself available to every student, conference participant, teleconference listener, and video viewer by personally taking phone calls and emails to answer any questions at any time. He has surely touched more lives in many ways than anyone I have ever known."

appreciation events, lunches, and education "that have become the hallmark of our firm's growth."

— Sid recommended focusing on a niche rather than being a generalist. Create a specialty within the firm.

— Sid also said to develop high touch relationships with clients. "Show the client that you care and they will want more."

A final tip on managing your practice: Always be thinking of ways to expand your existing service lines or introduce new services. There are many directions you can take. Table 2.2 is a sample of the many services offered by CPA firms today.

Table 2.2 Services of CPA Firms

Advisory	Audit & Assurance	Tax	Transaction
Performance improvement	Financial statement and internal control	Personal tax	Lead advisory
Risk management	Financial accounting and reporting	Business tax advisory	Restructuring
Operations	Finance operations and controls	Business tax compliance	Operational transaction services
People	Internal audit	Tax policy and controversy	Transaction support
Technology	Merger & acquisition	Transaction tax	Valuation and business modeling
Risk management	Systems processes and controls	International tax	
Capital projects	Regulatory compliance reporting	Tax accounting	
Forensics	Sustainable business solutions	Indirect tax	
Finance	International Financial Reporting Standards	State & local taxes	
		Transfer pricing	
		Valuations	
		Cost segregation	
		Trust and estate	

Becoming a Teacher

During their careers, many CPAs teach CPE programs for the AICPA, state CPA societies, other professional organizations, colleges, and other institutions.

Teaching CPE classes, conducting workshops and conferences, or participating in video recording programs or webinars is an opportunity for CPAs to

- give back to the profession;

- share their knowledge and skills;

- exchange information and ideas;

- develop communication skills;

- meet and network with other professionals;

- get exposure to prospective clients or employers;

- build a professional reputation; and

- find more teaching engagements, such as at local colleges.

From having been both a student and teacher and having recruited teachers for his CPE programs and workshops, Sid says the qualities of successful teachers include the following:

• *A passion for teaching.* If you have a passion for teaching, regardless of the subject, that passion will come through to your audience.

• *Deep knowledge of your subject.* By becoming an expert in a subject, you can be invited to participate in programs in which your expertise is valued. In the process, you can build name recognition—your personal brand—which can lead to new clients.

• *Knowing your audience.* Who is in your audience? CPAs from small firms? Perhaps a mix of small firm and big firm CPAs? Maybe some lawyers and other professionals? Planning your teaching program begins with your audience.

• *Being prepared.* Plan a program that will engage your audience, provide them with information that has immediate, practical value, and make them want to return to your next program.

• *Communicating effectively.* Present technical information in simple, clear language that your audience can understand.

• *Engaging the audience.* Ask questions, answer questions, provide short quizzes, and otherwise make your teaching a dialogue with your audience.

- *Getting feedback.* After the program, talk to people in the audience or e-mail or phone them later to ask how you performed and how you could improve.

The following are examples of how Sid's teaching—his CPA exam review course, his tax and other workshops, to name a few—have helped CPAs and other professionals learn and apply that knowledge to advance in their careers, meet the needs of clients, and grow their practices.

CPA Exam Review Course

While Sid was with Lybrand, the firm gave him a week off to prepare for the CPA exam. He was so grateful to Lybrand that after he passed the exam, he wanted to help others pass. So, he took his notes from an exam preparation class he had taken, did further research on taking the exam, incorporated his own ideas, and created a self-study guide for exam takers.

On three consecutive weekends, Sid also taught the tax part of an exam preparation course. The instructor who taught the overall course was weak on taxes, and Sid agreed to take over the tax portion. When the instructor suddenly died, his widow asked Sid to run the course. He protested that his expertise was in law, not accounting. "You're a teacher," she told him. "So teach." Thus began Sid's long career as a teacher.

Sid's CPA exam preparation course became the most popular of its kind in New York City. Such was the demand that before one class, the fire department was asked to help turn away people who had not registered in advance but were hoping to get in. Sid decided thereafter to offer two classes instead of one to accommodate demand. He also continued to work at Lybrand.

Among others who took Sid's course in its early days was the late Peter R. Scanlon, who, at the time, was a manager at Lybrand. "The firm told him he couldn't make partner unless he received his CPA certificate," Sid said. "He took my CPA coaching course and passed with flying colors." Scanlon later became partner and then chairman and CEO of the firm.

Educating Practitioners

Over the years, most of those who took Sid's course have passed the exam. Arthur J. Thielen, CPA, with Maginnis Knechtel & McIntyre, Pasadena, California, said, "I took a one-day class over 30 years ago and passed the exam the first time."

Some who took Sid's course went on to become leaders in the profession. One is Stan Goldstein, who started a CPA firm that became one of the largest in New York and, in 2007, merged with McGladrey and Pullen, a national public accounting firm. He recalled, "Sid and I met in 1961 when I sat for the CPA exam and took Sid's study course. Not only did my Brooklyn College friend and I both pass the exam, but John Tuchler received the gold medal for achieving the highest mark in New York State! Sid was outstanding as a teacher—thorough, clear, and caring. He exudes a love of the accounting profession which infects everyone in his presence."

Today, Sid often encounters former students from his CPA exam review class throughout his travels. His run-ins have occurred in various places, from elevators to conferences and workshops he conducts.

Sid's Probability Chart

Mike Miller CPA, Concannon, Miller & Co., P.C., Bethlehem, Pennsylvania said

> In 1963, when I joined Lybrand, Ross Bros & Montgomery in Philadelphia as a junior accountant, I was asked to take a CPA exam preparation course taught by senior accountants from the firm. I, and 11 other first year junior accountants in my class, were given a handout prepared by Sid, a tax manager with the firm. It was a probability chart listing all the topics that were on the CPA exams for about the last 10–15 years. You could clearly see the trend and knew where to focus.

> As I recall, Sid also was responsible for explaining how the essay portions of CPA exams were graded. The total point value for each question was closer to 150 percent than 100 percent. In other words, we were advised to get something written on each key point but not to dwell on getting every point completely right. This would take less time, and we could still get full credit for the question.

> I certainly believe Sid's teaching points were instrumental in 11 of the 12 of us passing the CPA exam the first time and the 12th person getting three of the four parts.

Sid's Workshops

Since his start in teaching with his CPA exam prep course, Sid has become one of the preeminent CPE teachers in the country, as many who have attended his classes, workshops and conferences will attest. After attending one of Sid's recent programs, Martin J. Kamerow, CPA, said, "In my 50 plus years of such programs this was by far the best." It was even better, he added, than the programs he and Sid taught about 40 years ago.

Previous participants to Sid's workshops often express gratitude for Sid's influence on their lives:

"My time is your time"

Gerard Schreiber Jr. is a CPA with Schreiber and Schreiber, Metairie, Louisiana:

"I have attended Sid's workshops many times and have received invaluable information that helped with my practice and taking care of the needs of my clients.

"In 1984. as a result of a revision to the code, it was necessary to add an amount for personal use of company owned autos on W-2 Forms. Sid covered this in depth. We would not have been able to do the forms correctly without this information and the practice aids included in the material.

"I have attended his individual and corporate workshops many times and have always been impressed with his ability to focus on the current needs of practitioners. He always has the latest news on tax legislation or IRS pronouncements. This passion for the profession has served as a guide for me in servicing my clients and my dealings with other professionals.

"Sid has always shown a concern to the needs of the participants. He always gave his contact information, whether at his New York office or his hotel room. As he says, "my time is your time."

Sid's help after Katrina

"Sid called immediately after Hurricane Katrina, expressing concern to all the Louisiana CPAs whom he knew. He put me in touch with Bob Castle in California who had experienced the Oakland Hills fires. Bob shared information with me to assist with casualty loss calculations. He also helped and advised me on dealing with the IRS in Washington on Hurricane Katrina matters. This proved invaluable to me and fellow Louisiana CPAs. This was another example of Sid's unselfish and lifelong commitment to the CPA profession.

"I continue to be amazed at Sid's ability to continue to provide for the needs of practitioners and the concern he shows for all who have attended his courses. There has been no one who has served the needs of practitioners, the AICPA, and the public as a whole for as long as Sid has. This is a lesson and model for us all to follow."

"Truly, the master was the humble servant"

Theodore J. Sarenski is a founder and partner of Blue Ocean Strategic Capital LLC in Syracuse, New York:

"My first recollection of hearing Sid was when I was a staff accountant in a public accounting firm. We were sitting in the darkened conference room watching the TV monitor as the VCR tape rolled. The announcer introduced Sid Kess and his federal tax update for 1982, a year of significant change. I was impressed by his enthusiasm for the topic but more so by his ability to discuss complicated topics in simple language that I, as a fourth year staff, could understand and apply. Watching partners of the firm listen and take notes during the presentation, I was also amazed at the knowledge Sid had since I thought the partners of the firm were so knowledgeable. Over a number of years I would continue to watch and absorb the lessons delivered by Sid as I tried to become a better tax accountant.

"Forward to 2009 and a meeting of the AICPA PFP Executive Committee, which Sid joined. Each time a new topic was discussed he had something to say. Have you ever been at a meeting where there is always a person who needs to comment on everything, and, sometimes it is just to hear themselves talk? This was not the case with Sid. New ideas, new approaches, marketing opportunities, and other suggestions were offered by him with the eagerness and energy of people half his age.

"November of 2011: I was asked by Sid himself to kick off his Sophisticated Tax Conference in Boston with a presentation on Social Security. Being introduced to speak by the man whom I first watched in the darkened conference room nearly 30 years before gave me goosebumps. Who was I to be sharing the stage with such a legend? Sid came up to me at the break and thanked me for coming to speak at his conference. It was not just a thank you. It was a warm, thoughtful, caring, sincere, and heartfelt thank you. Here was a man who could have walked away years ago with many deserved accolades, mentoring and teaching CPAs as if this were the first time he had been given the charge.

"Truly, the master was the humble servant."

Making technical issues understandable and interesting

Clark Blackman, CPA/PFS, is founder and president of Alpha Wealth Strategies, Kingwood, Texas.

"Sid Kess was an iconic figure in the CPA community long before I first saw him teaching at an income and estate planning conference in 1988. At the time, my job required the highest level of understanding of the issues surrounding income and estate planning for high net worth individuals. I was already aware of Sid's national reputation as a result of his prolific writing on the subject. He was (and still is today) truly the expert in sophisticated tax strategies for advisors on tax planning issues.

"At the conference, he did not disappoint. His deep knowledge and the energy and clarity with which he presented that knowledge affected me in a lasting and profound way. He deftly demonstrated how technical issues can be made understandable to the average person and communicated in such a way as to actually make them interesting! I can't think of any person who has had a more enduring impact on the technical development of individual tax and financial planning focused CPAs.

"More than twenty years after that conference, I had the incredible privilege of not only meeting Sid, but rubbing elbows with him as a fellow member of the AICPA Personal Financial Planning Division Executive Committee. He is a veritable font of ideas and enthusiasm and consistently sets the example of how volunteers can make a difference in their profession.

"The profession is better, the AICPA is better, and most certainly I am better for Sid's decision to share his incredible talents, making CPAs better tax planners, thinkers, and personal advisors."

James A. Seidel, J.D., LLM. Director, Federal Tax Content. Thomson Reuters Tax & Accounting Knowledge Solutions

Like many others, I caught the "tax bug" from Sid Kess. He taught my first federal tax course at New York Law School, and made what I expected to be a boring course that I felt obligated to take into a lively, relevant learning experience. Strange concepts like carryover and stepped-up basis became readily understandable. The importance of taxation in personal and business affairs came quickly to light. Sid made it interesting. That course set me on a path that led to an LL.M. in taxation from NYU Law and career in tax publishing. After a few years of experience at Prentice Hall and RIA, Sid hired me to edit Business Strategies, one of his CCH publications. And that opportunity to see Sid work up-close showed me how to deal with press inquiries, juggle multiple responsibilities, deal with high-level professionals, and most importantly treat people fairly and with dignity.

And that's the thing about Sid. Putting aside the incredible career he has had a leader of the tax community and the thousands of people he has taught for decades, what really defines Sid is his unfailing loyalty to those with whom he has worked over the years. When, with two partners, I started a professional editorial business, Sid was right there as our first client, helping us get over the hump to self-sufficiency. For years we worked with Sid providing current awareness materials for his annual AICPA individual and corporate tax updates courses. It was challenging and interesting work, and we were happy to have it and to continue to be associated with Sid. Sid also recommended my partners and me to many others, helping us develop significant business relationships with Maxwell Macmillan, Matthew Bender, CCH, and RIA. In the other direction, Sid has sent many tax people my way, and his recommendations are always very highly regarded.

What started as a student-teacher relationship and then a business relationship with Sid has become a warm, meaningful personal friendship. And that's the way it is with Sid. All the professional awards and kudos that he's garnered and so richly deserves never get in the way of what he's really about, which is helping people to learn and to prosper.

The Value of Sid's Workshops

In the mid-1960s, Sid became a road warrior, traveling thousands of miles annually across America to conduct AICPA-sponsored individual and corporate income tax workshops. He also conducted tax workshops for the New York State Society of CPAs. Later in his career, as a CPE lecturer, he organized, moderated, and spoke at other workshops.

Every year, for many years, he conducted 45 of the AICPA's two-day individual and corporate income tax workshops. Add a couple of days of travel time for each workshop, and he was spending up to half the year on the road. Not only that, but he also was responsible for managing the tax practice of Main Hurdman (later KMG Main Hurdman), where he worked with the firm's top specialists in different areas on tax issues, guided them on tax questions, pointed out tax planning opportunities, and assisted the firm in reviewing the returns of wealthy clients and verifying the taxes they should pay.

Practitioners could learn more in a two-day workshop with Sid than they could in weeks of research on their own, and his information and insights had practical value. They could immediately use what they learned from Sid to assist their clients, for example, to legitimately minimize their tax bills or avoid tax traps that could create compliance problems. Millions of taxpayers who never heard of Sid benefitted from being clients of practitioners who attended his workshops, took his classes or study courses, or read his articles and books. Sid also wrote articles and books for the consumer market, that is, individual taxpayers, owners of small businesses, and others.

Walter M. Primoff, CPA/PFS, director, Professional Advisor Group at Altfest Personal Wealth Management, and past deputy executive director of the New York State Society of CPAs, recalls attending a Sid workshop:

> Here was this inspired teacher, communicator, and coach, a "Big 8" CPA with a Harvard law degree, with a natural affinity for CPAs from local and regional practices.
>
> With uncommon intelligence, warmth, and wit, he taught us how to turn complex tax rules into planning opportunities, and then planning opportunities into marketing ones, enhancing CPA competence, profitability, and value to clients.

Primoff goes on to say that "a highlight of my career was Sid's singling out a new tax rule buried in the tax code and missed by a nationally renowned tax lawyer, enabling me to 'hit one out of the park' in front of the amazed attorney, our client, and my firm's managing partner."

How Sid Got Started Teaching His Tax Workshops

In 1964, Norman Auerbach, a Lybrand, Ross & Montgomery partner (and later, chairman of Coopers & Lybrand) became the chair of the continuing education section of the New York State Society of CPAs. He asked Sid to write, teach, and promote a tax workshop for the New York State Society of CPAs. "At the time, there wasn't any CPE to speak of, and my workshop was something of a novelty," Sid commented. It also was an instant success, with about 700 people attending the first one. Word spread and, soon, state CPA societies, as well as the AICPA, were contacting Sid. "I had a formula for success," he said. It was the formula he would use for years to come: know your audience, speak in terms they understand, and give them practical ideas they can immediately use to generate revenue.

Sid received $200 for teaching, writing, and marketing his first program. Upon learning of this, the head of the New York State Society continuing education Program told Sid, "You're a great teacher, Sid, but a very bad businessman." Sid and the AICPA agreed that if 100 people attended his first workshop, he would receive a minimum fee of $500. As it turned out, hundreds of people attended and, thereafter, Sid was paid a royalty based on attendance. Sid continued to conduct tax workshops for the New York State Society, which had provided the first opportunity to teach (for the original $200).

"...he taught us how to turn complex tax rules into planning opportunities and then ... into marketing ones"

Oscar Ornelas

I was first introduced to the "Sidney Kess, CPA, Esq" as an attendee to his individual and corporate tax seminars in the late winter of 1972. Amongst practitioners, "the Kess seminar" was considered the Cadillac of tax workshops, renowned for their depth, mastery of material, and proficiency. If you were a CPA attending the workshops, the value of your services would jump to a new level, and so, practitioners from across the United States would flock annually, like bees to honey. But it was in the lobby of a Houston hotel that I met "Sid, devoted father and friend." My wife and I were sitting with two fellow Texas attendees when Sid walked by headed to dinner. Prompted by my better half and Texan hospitality, I invited him to join us. The eyes of Texas smiled on the birth of a beautiful friendship that night.

Ironically, I owe my current office location to Sid. You see it was through one of his workshops that I learned of the "Rehabilitation Credit." The Tax Reform Act of 1976 added IRC $191, which gave birth to the Credit, giving optimal tax incentives towards the renovation of historic, income-producing real estate. Unsure of the Credit's survival in1986, I purchased a beautiful but ill-conditioned building with the hope of someday restoring it to its former glory. Well, it was through Sid that I learned of the Credit's survival, post-Tax Reform Act of 1986.' I was able to shorten its rehabilitation by the simple act of being able to afford it sooner rather than later. Twenty-five years later, that building still houses my practice and remains a talking piece amongst my clients.

Given the quality and proficiency Sid's seminar content, I subsequently began travelling with my wife, a proficient accountant in her own right, and two of my children, who went on to become CPAs. The same friendship we had fostered with Sid quickly duplicated itself onto our kids as well. When my son graduated from Texas Tech Law, he expressed a deep desire to pursue a Masters in Taxation. Having an excellent academic record proved insufficient to insure acceptance into NYU's distinguished LL.M. program. It was, indeed, Sid who proved instrumental in my son's acceptance into the Program as a member of the NYU Dean's Advisory Board. Throughout his stay at NYU, he enjoyed Sid's counsel and personal advice. It was a fortuitous friendship that both fostered—one that would prove life changing. During the terrifying attack on 9/11, all communication to New York became an impossibility. The nation fell silent, in sheer horror of the vitriol befalling our country. And if you were a parent, living 2,000 miles away unable to reach your child living but a mere 4 blocks away from Ground Zero? In truth, you felt your soul weep. The helplessness was indeed, unbearable. Luckily for us, my wife and

I were able to get word out to Sid, who was able to locate our boy. In the wake of 9/11, we as a family, were kept in touch altogether, with Sid acting as the conduit. Such gesture is borne out of sheer human decency. It is, undoubtedly, borne out of his understanding as a father, as a friend. My gratitude shall forever remain his.

Much to our dismay, Sid ceased offering his workshops. Forced to look for replacement seminars, we quickly discovered that other lecturers simply did not come up to Sid's standards. His knowledge, depth, and masterful teaching established him as the authority in tax across the United States. That's not bias—that's forty-seven years of experience talking. No one, man or woman, then or since comes close to Sid. No one is better versed in tax. How could they be? Sid is kept abreast, up to the moment, by the very people that negotiate and author our nation's tax laws. That is called authority.

Through the last 35 years, Sid has been more than a mentor to me and my family. He has been a part of our family. His work ethic and unsurpassed knowledge have justly earned him the respect of his peers and his profession. But his giving spirit, devotion to loved ones, candor and humanity have endeared him for a lifetime and beyond. For unto us, he is much more than "Sidney Kess, CPA, Esq." To us, he is simply "Sid Kess, father and friend."

"The tax law is even driving the bats batty!"

Sid Kess

Brief History of the Federal Income Tax

For more than a century, the United States managed its finances without an income tax. There were some short-lived exceptions, including a tax during the Civil War, but an income tax imposed during the 1890s was declared unconstitutional by the Supreme Court.

The 16th Amendment to the U.S. Constitution cleared the way for a federal income tax, and we've had one since 1913. The term *Internal Revenue Code* (code) came into use in 1939, when Congress acted to assemble all the various income tax laws into one comprehensive document. The 1939 code was the one that I learned when I went to college and then to law school.

The 1939 code was replaced by the Internal Revenue Code of 1954 (the 1954 act), which modified the former version by incorporating all the tax laws passed in the interim. The drafters of the 1954 act intended to make tax law more precise and specific. As the code changed, it became more important for practitioners to stay current. Attorneys and accountants increasingly attended seminars and conferences in which leading authorities on the new law explained its nuances.

Tax legislation continued with tax reform acts passed in 1969 and 1976. The next major change occurred with passage of the Tax Reform Act of 1986 (the 1986 act). In fact, that legislation officially renamed the code so that the Internal Revenue Code of 1954 became the Internal Revenue Code of 1986, which is where it stands today.

In pursuit of tax simplification, the 1986 act reduced the number of tax brackets. The top rate was lowered from 50 percent to 33 percent, and some tax deductions were trimmed. Perhaps most important, this law was designed to curb the use of tax shelters, which had attracted wide public notice. The proverbial shoeshine boy was not passing on stock tips; by the early 1980s, he was telling customers where to find a $10,000 investment that would generate a $30,000 writeoff.

(continued on pg. 48)

(continued from pg. 47)

New areas of specialization

Although tax simplification may have been a Congressional goal, that was not always the outcome. To stem the tax shelter tide, Congress passed the *passive activity loss* rules, which effectively created an entirely new area of the law in regard to the taxation of investments. These rules are so intricate that some practitioners now specialize solely in teaching about them and practicing in that area.

Other areas of the evolving tax code have attracted similar specialization. Section 199 of the code, created as part of the American Jobs Creation Act of 2004, describes the Domestic Production Activities deduction. This provision also has produced experts who specialize in its interpretation, as have the tax laws covering inherited individual retirement accounts and the generation-skipping transfer tax, for example. As of this writing, it is unclear how the tax provisions of the health care laws passed in 2010 will be implemented, but they may prove to be another area meriting extensive attention.

An ever-changing tax code requires continuing education, and I have been fortunate enough to teach many professionals and arrange meetings where such learning can take place. While it's always wonderful to acquire new knowledge, tax law can be especially difficult to grasp. I recall one meeting with over 1,000 attendees in Chicago's McCormick Place, when the people sitting in the audience were literally ducking from low-flying bats. As the *Chicago Tribune* reported, I told the crowd that "the tax law is even driving the bats batty!"

Timely Information

In the days before the Internet, Sid traveled with four suitcases bulging with news articles, reports of Congressional committees, proposed legislation, new tax rules, and, yes, some clothes. (Today those reports, articles, and other materials would travel as e-mail attachments—the big ones that choke Internet traffic.) Sid was—and still is today—on a first name basis with airport baggage handlers and hotel doormen, asking how they are doing, inquiring about their families, and giving them generous tips for handling his luggage. In addition to what he carried with him, Sid could also call people with whom he worked or volunteered to ask them for information, research, or other assistance. Those who helped Sid in some way, large or small, were sure to get a thank you from him in the form of a phone call, letter, or perhaps a listing in a conference program.

Through his contacts in Congress, Sid would have copies of new or proposed legislation or rules or rulings dispatched to him as soon as they were printed. This was not easy to accomplish in the days before the Internet, when the government sometimes couldn't print and distribute copies of documents fast enough to keep up with demand. But having these documents enabled Sid to present up-to-date information in his workshops. "I would read the reports of the hearings of House and Senate tax committees, read proposed legislation—the House version, the Senate version, the revisions worked out in committee—and other reports and documents of interest," he said. "I would stay up on all of this material."

Kurt Oestriecher, a CPA with Oestriecher & Company, CPAs in Alexandria, Louisiana said his father, Emile Oestriecher, CPA, recalled that a major law was passed the day before Sid was to teach a course. "Sid updated his materials that night for the changes instead of using a very acceptable excuse that since the law had just changed, he did not have time to update his materials. This type of dedication is what separates Mr. Kess from other knowledgeable instructors." (Further comments from Kurt Oestriecher can be found on p. 98.)

Across the country, CPAs, lawyers, and other professionals filled hotel ballrooms, conference centers, and other venues for his two-day tax workshops, with Sid speaking up to eight hours a day, reinforcing himself with cups of tea. During his workshops, Sid would not allow any questions; he had too much material to cover in the time allowed; However, attendees could ask him questions after the conference, call him at his hotel late in the evening, when he would make himself available, or even call him a week or month later. If he wasn't available, he would return their calls. For take-home, attendees were given a binder containing details of Sid's presentation, supporting material, a bibliography of articles, books, and other items of interest.

Elliot Stein, who has CPA practices in Florida and California and has known Sid since they both worked for Main Lafrentz years ago, has attended two of Sid's annual workshops for a number of years. "Of particular importance were the seminars' loose-leaf binders," he said. "They provided, and continue to provide, practical and useful information, along with our hand-written notes from Sid's and speakers' lectures and the question and answer sessions. Every time I called Sid, he, or the contacts he provided, were very helpful to my practice. Sid's sage advice over the years through his seminars and publications for the AICPA and CCH has made a tremendous difference in the success of my small firm accounting practice."

Those attending Sid's workshops mainly included sole practitioners or owners of small and medium-sized CPA firms, which account for most of the firms in the United States. Some CPAs from Big 8 (later, Big 4) firms were also in attendance. The clients of the small and medium-sized firms generally were individuals and owners of small or medium-sized businesses; those of the Big 4 firms included many of the world's largest corporations. Sid's presentations always were attuned to the interests of his audience. He explained the tax code, recent changes to the code, proposed changes, and new developments in tax law, regulations, and other topics in language that practitioners and others in the audience could understand.

Ed Slott, CPA, said, "I remember Sid covering the material, and then we would answer questions he provided in the workbook. Then Sid would go over the answers so we would see where we went wrong and truly understand the tax provision and how it applied. He also taught by using examples that we could all understand and learn from." Slott went on to start his own tax workshops, using Sid's approach. (For more, see his contribution beginning on page 74.)

Wherever he went, Sid invariably was invited back. Gary Scopes, the AICPA's director of international relations, recalls

> I first met Sid in 1974, when he did a tax workshop in Shreveport, Louisiana. I had just become the first executive director of the Society of Louisiana CPAs and hosting Sid's workshop was one of my first activities as the new chief executive. Back then, the only other staff was a secretary. Sid already was a legend, and the workshop was a sell-out, with a couple of hundred people in attendance. I took a personal interest in making sure that Sid's experience in Louisiana was hospitable, possibly for selfish reasons, because we wanted Sid back to do it again next year and the year after.

Over time, Sid's workshops and conferences have evolved into a collaborative effort, with Sid organizing and moderating a workshop and inviting CPAs, lawyers, and other professionals to join him. In his role of moderator, "he is not a figurehead, but rather, someone completely current on the subject matter," said Steven G. Siegel, JD, LL.M., president of Morristown, NJ-based The Siegel Group. "His questions and insights go to the heart of the issues being considered. In organizing the programs, he is a nonstop engine putting forth creative ideas that make the program a success." (Further comments from Siegel are on p. 95.) Sid has created additional workshops, including the AICPA Conference on Tax Strategies for the High-Income Individual and the AICPA Conference on Sophisticated Tax Planning for Your Wealthy Clients.

Whether he has presented workshops on his own or with others, Sid has adhered to the principles he prescribes for himself and others: know your audience, speak to them in plain English, and give them take-home value.

Chith Kala, CPA, who became a member of the AICPA's Private Companies Practice Section in 2010, has watched Sid's webinars. "Each and every one of them was clear, concise, and to the point. The information presented was very useful, presented very logically, and in a pleasant and agreeable manner. Kudos to Sid for doing such a wonderful job and making it possible for the younger generation to take interest in the field."

Next Generation

Some of the CPAs and other professionals who have presented at Sid's workshops got their start because he had seen them speak or had heard about them. He invited these people to move up to the national stage by participating in the recurring conferences and workshops that he moderates for the AICPA and other organizations. He chose these presenters for their communication, analytical, and technical skills and, today, they are among the nation's leading experts in estate planning, individual and corporate taxes, S corporations, health care, and state and local taxes. Sid has encouraged, supported, and advised them in their development as public speakers and experts and, in the process, has been training the next generation of CPAs and other professionals to share their knowledge and expertise as he himself has done.

What CPAs and Other Professionals Have Learned From Sid

Thanks, boss, for insisting I take one of Sid's classes

Scott T. Rhine is a CPA with Hinkle, Richter & Rhine, LLP, in Delray Beach, Florida:

I was a 22-year-old CPA candidate in 1975 when my boss and future partner (Thomas Workman, Jr., CPA) insisted I attend Sid's refresher courses on Individual and Business Taxation in Miami Beach because "it was the best stuff out there." At the time, CPE was just becoming mandatory in Florida, and I wasn't even required to take CPE, but Tom knew I would be a better employee for having taken Sid's class. Probably 500-600 people attended then, a very big turnout as Florida was still a small, but growing state.

I was enthralled by the depth and magnitude of all Sid shared with us during those two classes, and even more excited that I got to discuss a particular case in a one-on-one session during one of the breaks. I attended a number of Sid's classes over the years and always came away with something of great value.

Mark Plostock, CPA, CITP, said, "When I first entered the accounting profession over 40 years ago, my employer said, 'If you take only one tax course, then take a Sid Kess tax workshop.' I did just that and have always made it part of my CPE courses."

Helping with the exam, and more

Harry A. Mervish is a CPA in New York:

I met Sid in July 1964 when I enrolled in his Coach Course for the CPA Exam. His problem-solving technique was instrumental in my passing the exam. Throughout the years, I attended his annual Income and Corporate workshops, where he always gave tips on how to increase your fee income. He made himself available to his students all the time. I spoke to him over the phone, asking his advice on tax situations. When my wife and I were redoing our wills, I asked him to recommend an estate lawyer whom I used and recommended to clients.

An unexpected result of Sid's CPA exam review course

Linda Levine:

I met Sid more than 50 years ago when we both worked at Lybrand Ross Brothers & Montgomery. I was in the management services department. Mark Levine was on the audit staff and took Sid's CPA exam review course. Sid was most fond of Mark. Aside from his helping Mark pass the exam, Sid suggested that Mark call me because he felt the two of us were naturals. Sid was right. After my first date with Mark, I told my mother that I had met the man I would marry. It was the most wonderful thing that has ever happened to me. We were married for 50 years, until Mark passed away earlier this year.

I will always be grateful to Sid for all the happiness he brought to my life.

Sid

3

Be Imaginative and Act on Your Ideas

Some CPAs and other professionals stand out because of their extraordinary talent and professional skills, but what really distinguishes the very best in the field from others is the power of their ideas. They have the imagination, creativity, and insights to develop ideas that have practical value for their firms, clients, and professional colleagues, but more than that, they possess the resourcefulness and determination to act on those ideas.

Idea Guy

"More than anything, Kess is an idea guy, with all the enthusiasm of a triathlete," *CPA Magazine* observed.[1] From a very early age, Sid has demonstrated an exceptional talent not only for coming up with ideas but for putting them into action. Sid's talents and skills are numerous: vision, creative talent, writing and speaking skills, education and experience in accounting, law, and tax, energy and drive, discipline, and focus. Combine all these with marketing ability, and you can see that Sid can take ideas from concept to reality. "I wish I had a dollar for every idea you've given me," Joe Gornick, executive editor at CCH, once told Sid. "My kids' future college education would be paid for, without a doubt."

---

1   T. Steel Rose, CPA, "Lessons From a Tax Master: Sidney Kess," *CPA Magazine*, August/September 2010, www.cpataxmag.net/component/content/article/53-augsept/115-augsepcover.html.

The following is just a sample of the ideas Sid has developed in his career. Many others can be found throughout this book:

- In the 1960s, Sid helped CCH organize the first User Conference for CPAs in computer prepared tax returns, part of an effort to help CPAs adapt to emerging computer technology.

- At Lybrand, Ross & Montgomery, his first employer, Sid took some in-house tax courses. "The problem was that they were too legalistic for CPAs," he said. He suggested changing from a mainly code-oriented approach to a more accounting-oriented approach. The firm adopted his idea, and Sid later became the firm's director of tax training.

- Grateful that Lybrand gave him a week off to study for the CPA exam, Sid decided to give back by writing a self-study course for exam takers. He went on to start and teach a course on preparing for the exam that became the most popular of its kind in New York.

To this day, Sid continues to develop new ideas. "Wherever I am, I come up with ideas. I try to think of something that no one is thinking about."

Sid is not only very good at creating new ideas, but he also is very good about sharing them. Sometimes, he privately suggests ideas to others and lets them offer up the idea; and he always gives credit to others if they help him to develop ideas. "I do give credit to other people," he said. "What's important is that ideas are freely shared, discussed, debated, and, if they are plausible, put into action."

"Sid has a truly unique ability to think outside the box," said Bernard Krooks, of Littman Krooks LLP, New York. He serves with Sid on many advisory boards.

On many boards, the same ideas keep getting revisited year after year. Not if Sid is on the board. Countless times, Sid would have an idea that was not something we, on the board, had heard before. Initially, they didn't see things Sid's way, but after they thought about it a while, they came around. Sid just sees ideas and opportunities before others and is able to articulate them in a way that others understand, even if they didn't initially agree with them.

Sid approaches problems and challenges differently than most of us. He is not shy about sharing ideas that are innovative and exciting. More importantly, he has the skills to convince others of the merit of his ideas. This is truly a special gift.

Sid's approach is very much in the spirit of knowledge sharing and dissemination, and he favors the practice of the free exchange of ideas in today's world.

Active Life

Sid retired as a national tax partner of KPMG Peat Marwick in 1988. Although he does not maintain the same frenetic pace he used to (when he was traveling half the year conducting his tax workshops for the AICPA), he still leads a very active life. "Sid has achieved more in his 22 years of retirement than most people achieve in their careers," said Mark Plostack, CPA, who has been a panel member at some of Sid's conferences and a member of the Tax Hotline Advisory Board that Sid previously chaired.

Sid and his assistant, Rose Ann M. Beni, maintain an office in New York's Rockefeller Center. During his days at the office, he speaks frequently with family and friends, offers professional and personal advice, assists people looking for work and people with jobs to fill, writes, edits, and travels.

A native New Yorker, Sid enjoys talking, occasionally stopping to ask, "Are you with me?," to make sure you're keeping up. He seems to have so many ideas, thoughts, and observations that he needs to express them—to get them out—even as more are occurring to him. So listen carefully, and if you have something to say, jump right in.

Sometimes he'll ask, "Do you want to hear an anecdote?" It's a rhetorical question. He can't wait to tell you a story, like the time he traveled to New Jersey to assist a friend, Pat Verde, an elevator operator, who was in court on a matrimonial issue. (See A History of Helping, p. 10.) Another day found him in his office, talking to an advisor to wealthy clients, those with multimillion dollar investment portfolios. Sid talks to everybody, regardless of their station in life. Moderating a conference, or interviewing panelists for a videotape or webinar, he is calm, relaxed, and confident, and very enthusiastic about his subject. He has the demeanor of a college professor, but he's not lecturing; he's having a conversation. You feel like he's the go-to guy if you have a tax problem—or any problem.

Sid is still very much involved in conceptualizing, suggesting, sharing, testing, and implementing ideas. He generates many of his ideas in informal discussions with colleagues and friends, in formal presentations at workshops and conferences, while counseling a law firm, writing articles, or serving as an editorial advisor.

Long before Facebook or LinkedIn, Sid effectively created his own social network, sharing information, ideas, and experiences with those who attended his workshops, as well as with other CPAs and practitioners, friends, and colleagues. As time went by and more people learned from him, his network grew ever larger. He can tap into his extensive network to put people in touch with the best experts in the country to discuss tax, estate planning, and other issues. He also subscribes to a service that provides him with the names and titles of hundreds of federal government officials in Washington, DC. This allows him to provide the contact information of the appropriate official when someone calls asking whom in government to contact to request information or talk about an issue or problem. Imagine a government official picking up a phone: "Sid told me to call you." Enough of those calls, and officialdom will start asking, "Who is this 'Sid' guy?"

Sid continues to moderate conferences for CPAs, tax practitioners, and other professionals. On occasion, he holds seminars for judges to update them on tax laws and issues. At many of his conferences, Sid invites leading experts in pensions, estate planning, International Financial Reporting Standards, and other areas of expertise to participate. For a talk to the American Association of Attorneys and Certified Public Accountants, he invited along a speaker who discussed foreign bank account and disclosure rules.

Sid has no intention of slowing down. The following are just some of the activities keeping Sid busy these days:

- Sid was named of counsel to Kostelanetz & Fink, LLP, a leading law firm in complex civil and white collar criminal litigation and in tax controversies and trials. The firm also offers an active practice in tax advice, estate planning, wealth management, and whistleblowing.

- He is chairing the May 2012 AICPA Conference on Tax Strategies for the High-Income Individual.

- He recently ran a conference on Tax Practice & Procedures for Baruch College. "Baruch gave me a free education, so I volunteered to run conferences for them," Sid said.

- He contributed several articles to *Tax Streamer*, the New York State Society of CPA's magazine.

- He prepares a monthly Tax Tip column for the *New York Law Journal*.

- He was appointed consulting editor and member of the advisory board of the *Journal of Tax Practice and Procedure*, one of the many editorial and advisory positions he has held in his career.

Sid believes, "When you enjoy what you're doing, it's not work."

Sid As Career Planner

Of particular interest to Sid is assisting friends, colleagues, and others with finding jobs and managing their careers. Sid has been a career advisor and mentor to countless numbers of students, young people just starting their careers, professionals in mid-career, and those planning to retire or are already retired.

Despite the weak economy, hiring in the accounting sector has remained strong.[2] However, the job hunt can be challenging. "Young people today don't have as many opportunities, although accounting offers more than other careers," Sid noted. "The most important thing in this job market is to get your foot in the door." Not only recent graduates, but experienced professionals who may want to change jobs or who are looking for work, may find that the job hunt is taking longer than in better economic times.

The focus on immediate job needs is understandable, but, CPAs should not neglect long-term career planning, and students currently in accounting programs should be thinking about which of the many career paths in accounting interest them. Assuming the economy continues to recover, however slowly, hiring conditions in accounting could continue to improve, and CPA firms and other employers could step up their hiring of CPAs.

The following are a few of Sid's suggestions on career planning:

- *Self-assessment.* Career planning begins with a candid self-assessment. "Be honest with yourself. How good are you?" Sid said. How would you evaluate your communication, critical thinking, business know-how, problem solving, interpersonal, technical, and other skills?[3] What are your strengths and weaknesses? Ask friends or colleagues whose opinions

Retirement? What Retirement?

After he graduated from Harvard, Sid decided to join a public accounting firm, Lybrand, Ross Brothers and Montgomery, and he spent his career in public accounting. Now, in his 80s, he's found a new career: he's joined a law firm. He is of counsel to Kostelanetz & Fink, LLP, New York University. Among other responsibilities, he advises the firm on tax controversies. As noted in this book, he remains very active in the accounting profession and continues teaching and advising. He recently was appointed to the New York Tax Controversy Institute Advisory Board.

Sid notes that in today's CPA firms, people in their early 60s or even late 50s are reaching their firms' mandatory retirement age. He thinks firms are prematurely losing valuable talent by forcing people to retire at a relatively young age. In any case, CPAs who retire should not feel as if their professional lives are over. In fact, they have many choices. They can start a business, teach, work for a foundation, go into government service, or pursue other interests or activities and perhaps start a new career.

For the benefit of both the profession and society, the AICPA has developed a task force to explore how the profession can employ people who are at or near retirement who have skill sets and knowledge that can be useful.[*] In one initiative, the AICPA has joined forces with the Service Corps of Retired Executives (SCORE) in the Veteran Fast Launch Initiative to connect veterans with CPAs across the country.[**]

[*] "An interview with AICPA President & CEO, Barry Melancon, CPA," CPA Letter Daily, December 19, 2011.

[**] For more information on the AICPA's Veteran Fast Launch Initiative, go to www.aicpa.org/InterestAreas/ PrivateCompaniesPracticeSection/Resources/ USSBA/Pages/FastLaunchProgram.aspx.

---

2   "Accounting Industry Goes Hiring; Wages Gain Too," *CPA Trendlines*, December 2, 2011, http:// cpatrendlines.com/2011/12/02/accounting-industry-adds-to-payrolls/#more-16153.

3   Start Here, Go Places, CPA Skill. See www.startheregoplaces.com/why-accounting/cpa-skills.

Sid's Career in Publishing

A prolific writer and original thinker, Sid has authored many articles and books, scripted numerous video courses, and created various audio courses. He has leveraged his publishing ideas across platforms, for example, by turning materials produced for a workshop into a video course or book. He has refined ideas for a book on a broad topic, such as individual income taxes, into ideas for more books, such as one on the alternative minimum tax for individuals. He has developed ideas for books and video courses targeted to different audiences, such as individual taxpayers, corporate taxpayers, and tax practitioners. He has developed ideas for books for specific audiences. For CPAs, he has written books on tax planning for their clients and on managing their practices. He has developed ideas for clients themselves, such as a book on issues to address in forming a business.

The following is a look at how Sid has turned his ideas into finished products.

AICPA

Sid says he considers the tax workshops he has conducted for the AICPA to be among the most successful ventures of his career. He has written books for the AICPA that are used in his workshops. Some of these books have been published for many years, such as the *Individual Income Tax Workshop* (47 editions) and the *Corporation Income Tax Workshop* (46 editions). In addition, he has written or coauthored specialized books and courses for accountants and tax practitioners, including *Accountant's Business Manual, Managing a Profitable Tax Practice, Tax Research Methods and Techniques*, and *Tax Planning for the Closely Held Corporation*. He also has coauthored an e-book, *Advising Clients in Tough Times*. Sid has authored and moderated video courses for the AICPA, including the Individual and Corporate Tax Returns Workshops, Tax Planning Techniques for Individuals and Businesses Videocourse, The AICPA Experts' Retirement Insurance and Estate Planning Videocourse, The AMT for Individuals: Strategies to Escape Its Reach, and Paying for College: Tax Strategies and Financial Aid Videocourse. Some of his books and video courses have been tied to specific tax law changes. These include the

you value to offer their assessments. This self-evaluation should continue throughout your career.

• *Create a vision.* After you've taken a look at yourself, take a look at where you want to go. Where are you in your career? Where do you want to be in 10 years? Accounting is such a diverse field that some accountants are not aware of all the available career paths. Public accounting is the most popular path, and many accounting graduates start their careers here because it gives them broad exposure to clients in different industries and companies. But CPAs can also find rewarding careers in the corporate, government, or not-for-profit sectors; they can start their own businesses or they can teach undergraduate and graduate accounting courses. Within these broad sectors, they can specialize in, for example, management, financial, forensic, or tax accounting; internal audit; or information technology. Armed with the knowledge of different career paths, you can make informed career decisions. Your vision might be to become a partner with a Big 4 firm or maybe a small CPA firm; to become a CFO or CEO of a company or not-for-profit organization; or to start your own CPA practice or perhaps a business outside accounting, such as software development. As you progress in your career, your aspirations may change as a result of your professional experience, personal interests, or new career opportunities, such as in financial planning services. Because CPAs have portable technical, analytical, and communication skills, and accountants are in strong demand, they have flexibility in changing careers.

• *Plan how to achieve your vision.* Next, think about how you will achieve your vision. What are your goals? Everyone has different goals, but some common ones shared by most people are to

— find meaningful, challenging work.

— work with a diverse, interesting group of people who enjoy working together.

— work for an organization that offers learning opportunities, such as internal or external training programs, and opportunities for career advancement.

— work for an organization that provides financial security.

— work for an organization that provides opportunities to give back to the community, such as through employer-sponsored volunteer programs.

Achieving these goals starts with your current job. "Whether you are newly hired or have been in your current job for some time, do the best possible job you can," Sid said.

book, *Kess on Tax Legislation 2010: Tax Relief, Unemployment Insurance Reauthorization, and Job Creation Act*, the AICPA 2001 Tax Act Videocourse, and the 2003 Jobs & Growth Tax Act.

CCH

In 1965, CCH acquired a company known as Computax, which had developed an automated system to prepare tax returns. While at Lybrand Ross Brothers & Montgomery, Sid suggested to the CCH sales representative that handled the firm account that the key to the success of this acquisition was to teach the user how to complete the input forms. The representative contacted CCH's Chicago office, and they asked Sid to conduct a series of user conferences in various cities around the country. These programs proved to be an overwhelming success.

Sid went on to collaborate with CCH on a number of other ventures. One of his first projects was the production of audio cassettes on the 1969 Tax Reform Act. Other audio courses were prepared on areas such as 1040 preparation, estate planning, and S corporations. Other projects followed, including the CCH newsletters: *Tax Planning Review, Estate Planning Review*, and *The Executive Tax Review*. After these successful newsletters were developed, Sid came up with the idea for developing the *Financial and Estate Planning Guide*.

Sid considers the *Financial and Estate Planning Guide* one of his most successful publishing ventures with CCH. Originally, CCH did not have an estate planning publication other than a pamphlet, which sold well but was not as comprehensive as he thought it could be.

Then, in 1976, an opportunity presented itself. Sid had been approached by Bertil Westlin, former chairman of the board of editors at the Institute of Business Planning, a publishing company owned by William J. Casey. (Casey, who served in the Office of Strategic Services during World War II, later sold the company to become CIA director in the Reagan administration.) Westlin was interested in writing a book on estate planning for closely held businesses, but Sid didn't think it would sell in competition with similar books and seminars already on the market. "I told him there was a need for an inexpensive, basic guide on estate planning."

(continued on pg. 60)

(continued from pg. 59)

Sid and Westlin agreed to coauthor an estate planning guide covering different types of estate planning for businesses and individuals, for example, estate planning for closely held businesses or estate planning for married couples with children. Sid submitted an outline to Vernon Lusky, a CCH executive, who asked Sid how many copies of the book CCH could expect to sell. About 50,000, Sid replied. CCH decided to print only 15,000 copies and had to print more. In all, about 47,000 copies of that first edition were sold. CCH has continued to publish the *Financial and Estate Planning Guide*, now in its 16th edition.

Sid came up with an idea for a spinoff of the *Financial and Estate Planning Guide*, which was to expand it into the *Financial and Estate Planning Reporter*, a loose-leaf CCH publication in four volumes: Volume 1 included an expansion of the *Guide*; Volume 2 had copies of actual forms, clauses, and checklists used in financial and estate planning; Volume 3 had articles on estate and financial planning; and Volume 4 included the estate planning newsletter.

Another of his ideas was *Business Strategies*, which explored topics that confronted a business, such as forming a business, insurance, bankruptcy, sale of a business, and so forth. So, for example, when the area focused on bankruptcy, it would be analyzed from different perspectives: accounting, law, tax, and business strategies. In addition, practice forms were added in the appropriate portion of each section.

Warren Gorham & Lamont

When Sid was at Lybrand, Ross Brothers & Montgomery, he contributed to a book on federal taxes that was written by the firm and published by Ronald Press. Sid became friends with Arthur Rosenfeld, Assistant to the president of Ronald Press. Later, when Sid was with Main LaFrentz & Co., Alvin Arnold, a friend from Harvard and WG&L's general counsel, called to ask for Sid's assistance in helping WG&L, a Main LaFrentz audit client, in reaching the accounting and legal market. Until then, WG&L had been known mainly in the bank tax field. Sid arranged for Arnold and Arthur Rosenfeld, a Harvard Law School graduate and attorney, to meet for dinner that very evening. After they

Life-long Contact

Azriela Jaffe, MBA, M.A., Author

Ten years ago, I was seated next to Sidney Kess at a Boardroom Dinner. What a good decision that was for Boardroom, Inc., to make. I was there at the time because I had just come out with a new book about managing the complexities of mixed Jewish observance in a marriage and family. Sidney was so interested in my story that our connection did not stop there. He was genuinely concerned for me and my situation, gave me his phone number, and suggested we stay in touch. I have since learned that this has been a common practice throughout Sidney's life, and that he does indeed stay in touch with every person to whom he makes this suggestion.

Stay in touch was really an understatement. From that point on, Sidney called me every year, sometimes two or three times a year, to ask me how I was doing, and to inquire about the well-being of my husband and children.

I had shared with Sidney during that first meeting that my husband was then the CFO of a marketing company in Manhattan, and somehow, even though he must have a rolodex of thousands of people in his head, he remembered me and my husband.

Not long ago, Sidney's son asked him if he knew anyone with a good CFO background for a job opportunity in Brooklyn, and Sidney recommended my husband. One month later, my husband started a new job as the CFO for Omni Rehabilitation Services, the largest provider of Title I rehabilitation services to children in the New York City school district. This job was handwritten for my husband's talent and experience.

Recently, a phone call to Sid landed us another miracle. My brother, who previously worked for a CPA firm, was out of a job. He is getting married in a month.

We gave Sid a call, and he called a good friend of his whom he has mentored over many years, and there was the perfect job opening available for my brother in his friend's CPA firm. My brother started working there, and he loves the new job and the people he works with. Now, he will get married as a gainfully employed man. What a difference this means in his new life together with his bride. Just like it was for my husband, this job is tailor-made for my brother's skillset.

And all this came about, with the help of God, because Sidney never forgot my family and our first conversation at the table ten years ago.

met, Arthur joined WG&L as a vice president. Rosenfeld later became president of WG&L and, under his direction, the company diversified its product line into tax publications other than banking. "He made the company one of the leading tax textbook publishers in America," Sid noted. Rosenfeld went on to become president of Prentice Hall Tax & Professional Reference Publishing and, later, president of Maxwell Publishing, which took over Prentice Hall.

Sid also helped WG&L to gain more visibility in the accounting profession, such as hosting a conference on the 10th anniversary of the Accounting Principles Board (APB). Lee Layton, chairman of Main LaFrentz, and the APB's head, was moderator of the conference. WG&L later merged with Thomson Reuters. Sid also edited the *Kess Tax Practice Report*, a WG&L publication that was distributed biweekly. Sid also authored several books for Warren Gorham & Lamont.

BNA

Sid participated in several programs to help accountants and lawyers keep up on tax literature, an increasingly difficult challenge in the information age. He prepared a bibliography of the best books written by the top experts on different subjects, such as corporate reorganizations and pensions, which BNA distributed to practitioners. He subsequently expanded the bibliography into a book, *Find Your Tax Answer Faster*, which was published by BNA. It also published Sid's *A Practical Guide to Tax Planning*.

Other Publishing Ventures

Besides writing books for CPAs, tax practitioners, and other professionals, Sid also has authored, coauthored, or collaborated with writers in writing articles and books for the public. Among other publishing projects, he coauthored with Robert Metz of the *New York Times* a series of articles in the *Times*, "Cut Your Own Taxes and Save." The series also was syndicated to about 100 newspapers nationally and published in 1986 as a book. He was the consulting editor of American Express tax guides published in the late 1990s and early 2000s. He wrote the *Retirement Planning Guide* (3 editions) and the *1041 Preparation and Planning Guide* (10 editions, CCH Inc.) with Barbara Weltman.

How Sid Has Helped People Find Jobs

The business world uses recruiters, employment agencies, and online job sites and networks to connect job hunters with prospective employers. Sid's friends, colleagues, and new-found acquaintances have him to help make the connections.

Sid is often asked (and just as often, offers) to help someone with a job search. With his vast network of people in business, accounting and law firms, other professional services firms, and not-for-profit organizations, he has not only found jobs for people but has found the job that's right for them. He hands his business card to everyone just in case the recipient might have a job opening or be looking for a job.

The following are examples from Sid's experiences with job hunting:

• When a Harvard classmate told Sid he wasn't happy in his job as a controller of a leading retailer, Sid found him a position as CFO for a leading law firm. "The job was perfect for him," Sid said. "His whole life changed."

• When a lawyer friend experienced in working with brokerage clients told Sid that her firm had cut her hours to half a day, he contacted a former student who was an executive at a leading investment bank. It turned out the bank wanted to hire someone with a brokerage background. Sid's lawyer friend got the job.

• When Sid visited a dental office, one of the dentists mentioned that his son, a law graduate, was looking for work. Sid arranged an interview for him at a leading law firm. "Even if a person doesn't get hired, that interview gives them hope that a job opportunity will come along," Sid said.

• Sid's son, A.J. Kess, a lawyer, told Sid that a nonprofit organization that provides rehabilitation services to New York City school children had an opening for a CFO. Sid had a friend who was the CFO of a New York company, and he put the executive in contact with the nonprofit. The executive got the job, and it was a perfect fit.

"One of life's greatest blessings is to help someone find a job," Sid said.

Sid doesn't just help people; he asks people to help people. He asks everyone he knows to use their own networks to help people find work. "Many of the people I know have numerous clients and big networks," he said. "It is terribly important that we ask our clients if they are looking to hire someone."

How Sid Has Helped People Advance in Their Careers

Never lacking for ideas, Sid has suggested to lawyers, CPAs, and other professionals how they can apply their experience, talents, and skills to start careers, find career opportunities, or advance in their careers.

Sondra Miller became a judge

Sondra Miller is chief counsel to McCarthy Fingar, LLP, in White Plains, New York. She formerly was a New York State Supreme Court appellate judge and, before that, a New York State Supreme Court judge:

Sidney has had a remarkable effect on my career as an attorney and as a judge. Sidney and I met at Harvard Law School when I entered in the first class to admit women in 1950. Sidney was already a knowledgeable law student. He urged me to become involved with his pro bono concept, "The Phillip Brooks House," which provided inspiration and education to budding young lawyers and encouraged their pro bono work to benefit their communities. Sidney invited various community leaders and workers to speak to interested Harvard Law students about the needs of their communities and population and the importance of pro bono legal assistance to those populations. That work is the background and genesis of the Harvard Legislative Reference Bureau, which published a journal on legislation. The journal is still in existence at the Harvard Law School.

Return to the law

On a more personal level, Sidney provided a major bridge for me to return to the law after my absence from it while I raised my three children. I had enrolled in one of Sidney's fine courses on estate and tax law when Sidney spotted me carrying one of his enormous loose-leaf binders and learned of my intention to return to the law. Immediately, he invited me to serve on a prestigious panel whereby I would be joining Manhattan Surrogate Court Judge Marie Lambert, Sandy Schlesinger, Esq., and several other experts to talk about a subject about which I knew nothing. When I declined with thanks, he assured me that after he tutored me and after I read his books, I would be well prepared to advise the audience on how to choose an executor, the role of a trustee, and the importance of gift giving. With great trepidation, I did serve on that panel, and it was the starting point of my return to the law after several years away.

Asking Sid's advice

When I was asked years later to seek election as a judge in the Family Court of Westchester County, I had lunch with Sidney at our Harvard Club in New York and confided in him my concern: I had very little litigation experience. Sidney assured me that my on-hands experience in raising three fabulous children was invaluable experience to serve as a judge in family court and, indeed, any other court. I did serve on the family court for three years, the supreme court for three years, and was later appointed by Governor Mario Cuomo to the Appellate Division, Second Department, where I served for 15 years. In 2006, Judge Judith Kaye (then the Chief Judge of the New York Court of Appeals) appointed me to serve as the chair of the New York State Court Administration Matrimonial Commission (now referred to as The "Miller" Commission), where reform of the matrimonial law was recommended, some of which is now effectuated.

In addition to Sidney's invaluable mentoring advice, he is a most extraordinary and irreplaceable friend to me and to countless others.

How a CPA/tax attorney became a CPE instructor—and an author

Alan Zipp, a Rockville, Maryland CPA and tax attorney, says, "I cannot say enough about the influence that Sid has had on my career and my professional practice."

For more than 25 years, Zipp was an AICPA discussion leader, teaching the Sid Kess Individual and Corporate Income Tax Workshops. That work originated from a conversation with Sid.

After graduating with a master's degree in taxation, Zipp attended one of Sid's workshops. "I met with him during a break and asked him about a specific position he took in his material and in his lecture."

Apparently, my argument was persuasive, as he changed his position both in his oral presentation and in the written materials. Shortly thereafter, he asked me if I would like to join his group of discussion leaders traveling around the country teaching his income tax workshops every year. What an honor to represent Sid Kess before thousands of CPAs.

At a meeting of discussion leaders in New York, Sid taught me how to teach alternative minimum tax to CPAs in 20 minutes or less. What talent he has! I have never forgotten his tips and tricks in accomplishing that teaching technique. To this day, whenever I speak to CPAs, I use the Sid teaching techniques. I always receive excellent evaluations using his methods.

In 1983, during a meeting with Sid to discuss certain divorce taxation issues for the Individual Income Tax Workshop, I gave him a copy of my master's thesis on divorce taxation. He said it was well written. The next thing I knew, I received a call from an editor at Prentice Hall, who said that Sid told them they should talk to me about publishing a book on divorce taxation. With Sid's influence, in 1985, Prentice Hall published my book, *Handbook of Tax and Financial Planning for Divorce and Separation*.

In 1990, I received a phone call from a *Money* magazine editor, asking me to prepare their annual Money Magazine Tax Test to be given to some 50 professional tax return preparers. The editor said Sid recommended me. I wrote the test, and it appeared in the March 1991 edition. That tax test had the largest spread of tax results in the Money Magazine Tax Test history.

For many years, Sid has invited me to participate as a panelist in his AICPA videos for self-study of his Individual and Corporate Income Tax Workshops. What a wonderful opportunity to serve on such a distinguished panel of experts, discussing tax topics with Sid Kess.

Because of Sid Kess and the opportunities he made available to me, the AICPA asked me to write a training course on business valuation. My course, Business Valuation Methods, was the leading AICPA course for self-study for more than 10 years. I prepared the course exactly as Sid Kess did for his tax workshops. He taught me how to teach professionals professionally. Without Sid Kess' guidance in CPE course preparation, I would never have succeeded with the business valuation course. Then, the AICPA asked me to write a case study CPE workshop in business valuation. Using my training from Sid Kess, together with a litigated divorce case involving business valuation, I prepared the very successful AICPA CPE course, Small Business Valuation Case Study.

Sid is my friend and my mentor. I am but one of the thousands of stories of the influence Sid Kess has had on the careers and personal lives of CPAs all over this country. He will always be among the most influential people in my life.

How Sid's workshops helped a CPA in law school

Eliana Sachar is a CPA and attorney in Washington, DC:

I had never worked in accounting when I studied for the CPA examination. My work experience in business was overseas, and I was not familiar with the U.S. tax code. But I took a CPA preparatory course and won the Elijah Watt Sells Award for the top grade among candidates sitting for the examinations in the state of Maryland.

I went to work for a large accounting firm in Washington, DC. I was assigned to prepare individual tax returns—this was in the days before computers. The firm enrolled me in the two-day AICPA 1040 workshop, which was given by Sid Kess. As a good student, I sat in the front row, listened attentively, took notes, and may have asked a question or two. During the lunch break, I introduced myself to Sid. He was surprised to learn that I was married to a former classmate of his at Harvard Law School. (My husband dropped out of law, earned his PhD degree at Harvard, and went on to become a history professor and an author of 20 books.) I was impressed with the clarity of the course material and Sid's manner of instruction. For example, he drilled us with questions at the end of each section. After the workshop, I felt I was ready to tackle the preparation of tax returns.

Since then, I have attended Sid's annual updates, and when I became a tax manager at another Washington accounting firm, I also attended Sid's annual corporation tax workshops and sent some of the office staff as well.

I am amazed at how Sid not only keeps up with the constant changes in tax law, including recent tax cases, but also is very knowledgeable about possible changes proposed by Congress.

I have attended the UJA-Federation of New York seminars that Sid has organized and that dealt with estate planning and philanthropic giving. These were very useful when, in mid-life, I attended Georgetown University Law School. Since graduating, I have specialized in tax and wealth conservation.

The material I obtained in Sid's seminars, as well as books on estate planning, were very useful resources that I could look up throughout the year. In his seminars, Sid emphasized current issues that accountants and lawyers needed to know and that had not been covered in many published articles.

Sid's teaching really stuck with me. There were times when I had to instruct my office staff on the preparation of tax returns. Since Sid had explained the material so clearly, my task was made easier.

Sid's teaching changed my life. I also appreciate his friendship, his concern for people, and his willingness to promote the interests of professionals.

"Sid was immensely supportive of women in the accounting profession"

Helena Rosenwasser worked with Sid at Main Lafrentz:

Sid's accomplishments are very impressive, but they are not reflective of his essential quality. His essential quality is his concern for other people.

I first met Sid Kess in the summer of 1970, when I was hired straight out of college by Main Lafrentz to work on the audit staff. Sid was the partner in charge of the firm's National Tax Practice.

During the orientation process, Sid spoke to the "newbies" about recent developments in tax. He talked about how the audit staff needed to be aware of tax issues and should be on the lookout for tax pitfalls during the audit process.

At the conclusion of the seminar, Sid asked me whether I would like to assist in the National Tax Office on some projects. Of course, I agreed. I must mention that in 1970, I was the only woman hired for the audit staff. The only other woman on the audit staff was an exchange accountant from one of the firm's German offices. The only professional women employed in the firm worked in the small business group.

Sid was immensely supportive of women in the accounting profession. There were still people in the profession who viewed accounting as a man's job. Since Sid's wife had started her career on the audit staff of a Big 8 CPA firm, he was aware of the difficulties that women encountered in entering the profession, even at that time.

At the time, Sid was writing a book about the 1969 Tax Reform Act. My formal tax education was very limited. Nevertheless, he was willing to give me the opportunity to work on the project. He showed me the tax library and was able to explain how the tax service was organized and how to find cases and rulings in 10 minutes or less. That is why Sid is renowned as the premier tax educator.

Sid was the original multitasker. He would come into the office in the morning carrying a suitcase containing the work he did at home. Besides writing his book on the Tax Reform Act, he also designed forms to be used by the firm's various offices' tax practices. He also wrote and conducted workshops, taught classes, and spoke to several of the firm's offices.

Sid Kess was a one-man benevolent association for the profession. People who needed work, people who got sick or down on their luck, all called Sid for help, and Sid did help them. Every morning, his secretary opened mail from individuals asking for his help. As an example, Sid received a letter from a Harvard Law alumnus (whom he had never met), who had lost his position as the editor of a well-known tax publication. Sid hired him to assist on his book project.

Over the years, I have met many people who tell me they are friends of Sid's. People who attended his workshops, his CPA review course, and those who have lectured with him, worked for him or with him, all have become Sid's lifelong friends. I am proud to call myself a friend of Sid Kess.

From comptometer operator to senior assistant tax specialist

Beatrice Lemlein retired from KPMG as a senior assistant tax specialist. She started her career as a comptometer operator:

I first met Sid in the early 60s at Lybrand Ross Brothers & Montgomery, where I worked in the Report department. At the time, tax returns were typed. People in the Report department would do the proofreading, check spelling, additions, calculations, and make sure that the schedules tied in to the various line numbers on the tax return.

I operated a comptometer (which was a glorified adding machine), as well as a Monroe calculator to verify that the numbers were correct. After several years at Lybrand Ross Brothers & Montgomery, I moved on to Main Lafrentz, where Sid had become national director of taxes. Sid knew me and my work ethic and felt I was so precise and meticulous in my work that I would be terrific as a return preparer because of the unique skill I had acquired earlier in my career.

He persuaded me, and several other ladies, to take a correspondence course to get a better understanding of tax principles and return preparation. After completing this course, I started working on tax returns for high net income individuals, and I continued doing this. After several mergers, Main Lafrentz joined with KPMG.

I worked for about 35 years preparing tax returns, meeting with clients, and dealing with IRS agents. Sid had always felt that a good mind focused on learning could do anything. Sid changed my life from being a comp operator to being a senior assistant tax specialist at KPMG.

I will always be grateful to Sid for being my mentor.

A career in publishing—with Sid's help

When Fran Davis was head of CCH's federal tax products, Sid was "a constant resource and reliable friend," she said. After she left the company, "I expected to be the youngest full-time retiree on record."

Sid had other ideas.

Within weeks, I was on the road to a fruitful freelance career through Sid's introductions to a number of tax publishers. One of those, the AICPA, offered me a full-time job when it transferred its continuing education arm to Texas. There, I managed Sid's landmark courses among the array of products. While Sid did not come along with those products, I knew he remained just a phone call away.

Throughout the publishing field—be it topical publishing, freelance, or continuing education—Sid is a proven idea person, creating new products and new learning tools for the practitioner. As many will attest, his ability to bring talented people together is the bedrock of excellent products and excellent careers.

Sid's professional counsel and personal friendship have played a most important part in my life, and for that I am forever grateful.

Fran worked at the AICPA until she retired.

Helping father and son with their careers

Richard A. Oshins is an attorney with Oshins & Associates, LLC, in Las Vegas:

Sid is a very special person and, indeed, a legend in the tax field. I first met Sid as a young lawyer in the 1970s, when he was lecturing and educating other tax advisors, sharing his vast wealth of knowledge. I believe that I became a much better lawyer learning from Sid. He is a legend as an educator. However, this opportunity to prepare a tribute honoring Sid is not only about Sid's vast accomplishments as an educator but more to express my feelings about Sid as a person.

Sid has been a mentor to me and my family in many ways. When I have been fortunate enough to be selected as a member of his faculty, my wife, Carol, and I have looked forward to the speaker dinner because it would give us the opportunity to spend time visiting with Sid. Sid is an extremely compassionate and caring man. When my son, Jason, was starting his career in financial and wealth planning, Sid met with him and counseled him. To this day, when Jay goes to New York, or Sid is in Las Vegas, he tries to meet with Sid.

I remember discussing Sid with my close friend and another iconic figure in the tax and wealth planning community, Professor Jerry Kasner. I can remember Jerry being asked to speak at seminars that Sid ran and rearranging his schedule because he could not say no to Sid. That is symbolic of the respect that Sid has in our wonderful profession.

Another illustration of how gracious Sid has always been is that when Sid chaired programs in Las Vegas, he always invited some of the firm's lawyers to attend. The knowledge they obtained from the training was substantial; however, that substantive knowledge pales in comparison to the opportunity to meet such a remarkable, scholarly, thoughtful, kind, gracious, charismatic man, who always exhibits the utmost integrity and dedication. To know Sid is an utterly rewarding experience. I am so pleased that our younger lawyers had the opportunity to experience that.

I also am fortunate to have observed how Sid has dedicated his life to improving our profession in so many other ways. We are on many advisory boards together. Sid's signature approach has always been, "What can I do to help?" Each professional organization is far better as a result of Sid's involvement.

Despite the numerous accomplishments in Sid's career as a scholar, a teacher, a mentor, a chair person, he has always remained compassionate and humble. His humility is illustrated by the fact that he is always extolling the virtues of others, never himself. Anyone who has met Sid has had their lives improved by that opportunity. And, Sid, thank you for the gift of your friendship.

Role Reversal

Lenny Berk

Sidney Kess recently reappeared in my life in what you might call unusual circumstances. I was the teacher, and he was the student. But more about that later.

I first encountered Sid Kess when he was teaching a CPA coaching course back in the 50's. I had already passed the first three parts of the CPA exam but was having difficulty with that last part. I had always had difficulty with cost accounting, and I heard that Sid Kess was teaching the "T" account method for problems in job order cost and process cost accounting. I enrolled in the course, and with his special help, I finally passed the last part of the CPA exam. I became a CPA, the crowning achievement in my life up to that point.

I practiced accounting for the better part of 30 years as a partner in a variety of small CPA firms. Every year around tax time, I would enroll in Sid Kess's annual tax review course. There were many courses out there, but Sid's was the best.

At the age of 59, after a lifetime of debits and credits, audits and taxes, I decided that enough was enough. I decided to sell my partnership interest in the firm in which I was a partner at the time and, instead, do something I loved. I had always been a people person and a foodie. I had cooked Chinese food in my elaborate kitchen at home and taught Chinese cooking as well.

I decided to create, direct, and lead gourmet dining tours to Asia in a company of my making with the help of a large travel agency, the president of which was a close friend of mine. In this endeavor, I spent three wonderful years going back and forth to Hong Kong, Thailand, and other parts of the East dining in the best restaurants and staying in the best hotels of the day.

One day, a close friend of mine called and told me that she saw an ad in the *New York Times* in which Zabar's, the ultimate gourmet food emporium in New York City, was advertising for a part time lox slicer. I thought, "I could do that." I applied for and secured the job. I have been slicing smoked salmon and dealing with all kinds of smoked fish now for 17 years. It is a labor of love.

That's where Sid Kess comes back into the picture. He used to come into Zabar's quite frequently to buy lox for his aged aunt, who died at 100 years of age. Even after her death, he continues to buy it for friends and for others less fortunate than himself. Now I slice his salmon, always giving him many tastes along the way, as he watches and admires how I slice the lox and lay each slice on parchment paper while he tells other customers standing alongside that I was his student way back. Some of them look a little confused, not knowing who he is, probably thinking that my entire life has been spent with smoked fish.

4

Maximize Your Potential

"Maximize your potential." It's advice that people hear from a very early age. It's given by teachers to students, mentors to those they are mentoring, and experienced CPAs to those just starting out.

To maximize their potential, CPAs and other professionals often focus on a specific goal, such as maximizing their potential as auditors or tax practitioners, and they have a plan for achieving that goal, and measuring their progress. In focusing on a specific goal, or a limited number of goals, however, CPAs may be overlooking opportunities to fully develop their potential in other areas. One is practice development.

CPAs and their firms may not always have the time to devote to practice development, which includes things like public speaking, writing and editing, and media relations, because of the pressures of serving clients, managing a practice, and so forth. CPAs may not place much value on these "soft" skills; but practice development has direct benefits, including the following:

- *Market exposure.* CPAs and their firms gain exposure with key audiences, which include clients, prospective clients, current and prospective employees, professional societies, decision-makers in business and government, and reporters and editors.

- *Branding.* Firms can enhance their brand recognition in the markets they serve, such as small businesses.

- *Thought leadership.* Skills such as public speaking and writing establish CPA firms as thought leaders on the cutting edge of ideas, innovation, and best practices.

- *Networking.* CPAs and accounting firms can develop contacts and build broader and deeper networks.

- *Communication skills.* CPAs can develop and refine their communication skills through speaking and writing.

With Sid's help, some CPAs and other professionals have discovered that they have potential as public speakers. Sid has helped them to realize their potential by inviting them to join his panels on tax and other subjects, or by helping them to get on other panels. He has also advised them on developing their speaking abilities.

Public Speaking

Anyone who has heard him speak knows that Sid is an accomplished public speaker. He started in high school, when he chaired various student organizations, started new ones, and led fund-raising drives. Sid has given thousands of presentations at conferences, workshops, conventions, classes, and other venues, as well as having moderated or been a panelist on hundreds of video recordings and webinars. He has also advised, assisted, and supported other professionals in their development as public speakers. The following are a few of Sid's suggestions to help CPAs and other professionals with public speaking:

- *Speak at every opportunity.* Whether it's a meeting with a few people in your company or a luncheon meeting for several hundred people, take every opportunity to speak in public. It doesn't matter if you are a CPA with 20 years of experience or a college student. Many opportunities exist for speaking publicly. CPAs can speak at meetings with a few other practitioners or employees, company luncheons or dinners, training workshops, and, once they develop their skills, at presentations to clients. Likewise, students can speak in the classroom, at meetings of student organizations, and at school events. Professionals and students alike can volunteer to serve community organizations, civic groups, professional societies, and charitable organizations.

- *Be a leader.* Public speaking provides excellent opportunities to simultaneously develop your leadership skills. At work, offer to chair committees, task forces, and working groups. At school, volunteer to lead student organizations and events. In the community, offer to head up organizations, meetings, and work days. Or, start up an organization, committee, or task force at school, work, or in the community where you see a need and have an interest. "Get involved in different groups," Sid advises, "and don't be hesitant about chairing the group."

- *Know your audience.* It's a Sid mantra: know your audience. An audience of CPAs who are sole practitioners or belong to small firms may have different interests and expectations than CPAs from the largest firms. Lawyers may have different expectations than CPAs, and students may have different expectations than experienced practitioners. By knowing your audience, you can craft a presentation that captures their interest and avoid the mistake of speaking on topics that have little interest. Sid gives this example:

> If you are a professional with extensive experience in working with international clients, but you are speaking to an audience of small practitioners, you could assume, or find out beforehand, that each has one or two international clients or are interested in working for such clients. Then you might talk about the ins and outs of doing business in the global market, the opportunities and risks, and some of the legal aspects.

- *Be prepared.* Do your research. Think of ideas to present. Ask others for their ideas, and give them credit during your presentation. Test out your ideas with others. Ask their opinions. The better prepared you are, the more comfortable you will be speaking. "I was always prepared with ideas, so I never had stage fright," recalls Sid.

- *Be organized.* Whether you have a printout of your complete presentation in front of you or a few notes with your key points, think about how you will structure your speech, raise issues, present your ideas, and offer solutions.

- *Think local.* When he was traveling the country to conduct his tax workshops, Sid always prepared in advance by having the local newspapers sent to him, talking with local CPAs and others, and otherwise developing market intelligence. "It's very important to talk about the local community," he said.

- *Be yourself.* Whether you are speaking to a few people in a room or several hundred people at a workshop, be yourself. You are having a conversation with your audience, not giving a lecture. Be honest, forthright, candid, and attuned to your audience.

- *Don't pretend.* Don't pretend to know something when you don't. Don't put information in your speech that you haven't researched or verified. If

How Ed Slott Used Sid's Workshop Teachings to Build His Business

Ed Slott, a CPA in Rockville Center, New York, developed his public speaking, writing, and teaching skills to build his CPA practice, establish his reputation as an expert, write books, and provide training to advisors in individual retirement arrangements and retirement distribution planning. He is the founder of irahelp.com.

Before I got to know Sid Kess, I knew him only as a tax expert, when I attended his many CPA tax programs. After I finished college and got my first job with a small accounting firm, my father (who was also a CPA with his own small company) took me to my first Sid Kess tax workshop. He attended them religiously and made sure that I did too.

I always looked at Sid as the all-knowing tax master. But what I really took from him is that I finally went to a CPA tax program where I understood and learned through Sid's workshop teaching methods. I remember Sid covering the material, and then we would answer questions he provided in the workbook. Then, Sid would go over the answers so we would see where we went wrong and truly understand the tax provision and how it applied. He also taught by using examples that we could all understand and learn from. I use that approach today in my own programs.

He spoke in a down to earth manner, and I found this amazing since no one else was really doing anything like this back then. And still today, nothing compares to Sid's workshop teaching methods. Sid showed CPAs, especially small firm guys like me, how to understand virtually everything we needed to know about preparing personal and corporate tax returns. He set the gold standard.

It was about that time that I realized I wanted to do that as well—both to learn more and to build my business and my presence as a knowledgeable CPA. I looked at Sid as the high mark to achieve, but also realized that no one would ever

you are asked a question and don't have the answer, say so, but follow up by finding the answer and getting back to whoever asked.

- *Be practical.* Sid recalled that Norman E. Auerbach, who started as an accountant at Coopers & Lybrand and later became its chairman, always took a practical approach in his presentations in a classroom, at a meeting, or at an event. He gave the broad picture on a subject (for example, consolidated returns) and left the discussion of the details for another speaker, at another place and time, for those who wanted more information. By contrast, some speakers dwell on details to the point that they lose sight of the big picture and lose their audience.

- *Create take home value.* Another Sid dictum: "Always leave your audience with a few ideas that they can take home and put to immediate use." Display them on a screen or include them in a handout. Audiences want ideas that they can put into action.

- *Collaborate with others.* Sid has often collaborated with other professionals on articles, books, courses, training materials, workshops, conferences, videotapes, and webinars. He values collaboration as a means to

— share the work;

— draw on the talents of others;

— get their views and opinions;

— complete projects faster;

— improve the quality of the end product;

— provide experience to those who have not collaborated on many projects;

— train people in helping to manage projects; and

— show what can be accomplished through teamwork.

"A cardinal rule of collaboration is to always show people that you value their contribution," Sid commented. Tell them personally. Give them credit in a book, article, or other published material. Thank them publicly at a workshop or conference.

Chuck Levun, a partner of Levun, Goodman & Cohen, LLP, in Northbrook, Illinois, was a speaker at the 2010 AICPA Tax Strategies for the High-Income Individual conference in Las Vegas that Sid organized. "I very much appreciated the glowing introduction Sid gave me, the specific mention of the programs that I presented and sponsored, and his excellent feedback on various aspects of my presentation. He is an excellent role model for me and for other attorneys and CPAs who spice up their careers by speaking to, and writing for, professional groups."

Collaborating

CPAs can maximize their potential by collaborating with other CPAs and other professionals on endeavors of common interest. Collaboration enables CPAs to achieve goals that they might not be able to attain on their own and

compare to the amazing Sid Kess. To me, he was up on an unreachable pedestal.

He gave me the incentive to get involved with both the AICPA and my state CPA society (the New York State Society of CPAs). I got involved and joined committees. I took a special interest in estate planning, since the laws in that area were going through major changes at the time with the Economic Recovery Tax Act of 1981, known as ERTA.

Among other key provisions, ERTA gave us the unlimited marital deduction and the QTIP provisions* still used widely in planning today. It also raised the annual gift exclusion to $10,000 from $3,000, another major planning tool we still use today (now it's $13,000 in 2012).

I realized that this was an area that, at the time, most CPAs (or at least most small firm CPAs) were not addressing with their clients even though these new provisions would affect most clients' estate plans. So I wanted to learn even more.

Of course, it was Sid Kess, who, a few years later, wrote one of the best books on this topic—so I could understand it. Attending his training became even more valuable, since there was so much new tax planning material to understand and put to use.

Another big tax event was in 1987, when the first IRS regulations were released (from the 1986 Tax Act) on IRA and plan distributions, also known as "The IRA Distribution Rules." These were some of the most complex provisions of the tax code, and they applied—or would soon apply—to virtually everyone with retirement savings. Yet, this was an untapped area for practitioners.

With the help of IRA expert Seymour Goldberg, who I believe saw this opportunity before anyone, I decided to gain expertise in this area and create a planning niche. I authored several books on the topic, which eventually lead to training other advisors. I still do that today.

But the biggest breaks came because of Sid Kess. I don't remember how he even came to know of me, but I do remember the day I got the first call from Sid Kess. I could not believe that Sid Kess was calling me for anything.

Here is a guy I looked up to and

(continued on pg. 76)

(continued from pg. 75)
respected from afar, like every other CPA who attended his courses or read his books. The first thing I did was tell my dad that Sid Kess called me. He said "*The* Sid Kess…from the tax courses? Wow!" I felt like a made man, for a CPA anyway.

Sid had called to invite me to speak at one of the most prestigious AICPA conferences, Tax Strategies for the High-Income Individual in Las Vegas.

I cannot describe how great that made me feel. I could not wait to present at the conference. I still remember that I presented a program on Income in Respect of a Decedent. During the program, Sid popped his head in to check on me and gave me that nod.

He spoke with me later about my presentation and made me feel like I was the only presenter at the program, even though there were over 20 other speakers. But that is what Sid does. That is the absolute magic of Sid Kess. I learned that again over time, as Sid included me in even more programs, always promoting me and calling me to see how he could help me. Who does that? No one but Sid.

He still does that today. When Sid calls, the first questions have nothing to do with taxes. He usually asks, "How are you?" or "How can I help you?" I thought he just took an interest in me at the time but, over the years, I came to realize that he does this for everyone. He finds a way to help anyone he can. He is always generous with his time.

I learned from Sid that success lies in helping others get what they want, and I try to follow his example with everything I do.

When I first started writing books, it was Sid who introduced me to major media sources, like Jan Rosen, the distinguished *New York Times* financial writer. Ms. Rosen eventually gave me a great blurb for my book and even helped me improve the writing—all because of Sid Kess.

I still have my CPA practice, but now I mainly do advisor training programs in the

to realize other benefits of collaboration, for example, in writing books.

Book Projects

In 1970, when he was the national tax director at Main Lafrentz & Co., Sid collaborated with the firm's offices in writing a book, *The Tax Reform Act: A Manual for Tax Practitioners*, about the Tax Reform Act of 1969, which the preface to the book described as "probably one of the most significant, complex, and far-reaching laws enacted in the past 50 years." Professionals in the firm's offices wrote sections, and Sid edited the manuscript. About 50,000 copies of the book were sold, far exceeding the expectations of the firm and the publisher, Warren, Gorham, & Lamont. Sid made sure that everyone in the firm who participated in the project got credit in the book. The book's success helped to give Main Lafrentz a higher profile as a national firm.

William H. Behrenfeld is a CPA and tax attorney in Sarasota, Florida. In 1970, he was a tax manager in Main Lafrentz's New York office and a contributor to Sid's book:

I submitted my section and had the opportunity to review many of the manuscripts that were sent to Sid for his review and revisions. I must say that, at that time, the material was very boring.

I was amazed at the job Sid did in revising the manuscript by clarifying many of the sentences, adding explanations, quizzes, and boxes that highlighted the new law. I then realized this man was a genius and had the ability to simplify very complex rules and give examples of how the new law worked.

In my 52 years of practicing law and accounting, I have met only one other professional who had the same ability as Sid to simplify the Internal Revenue Code so that a lay person would understand it. His name was Arthur Dixon.[1]

Knowing Sid's ability to make the tax law interesting and to market his published material, I was very fortunate after 40 years to again be working with Sid on the AICPA publication, *Accountant's Business Manual.* I now have my son, Craig, working on this book with me, so that he also would learn from Sid.

For another book that Sid wrote, *Managing a Profitable Tax Practice: Text, Forms and Procedures*, published in 1972 by Warren Gorham & Lamont, the California CPA Foundation asked hundreds of practitioners throughout California to participate in a survey and share with other professionals the forms, questionnaires, checklists, bulletins, and other documents they used in their tax practices. The purpose of the survey, and the workshop programs that followed it, was to explore how to increase the profitability of firms. Other practitioners, including the partners and tax network of Main Lafrentz & Co., also contributed. "Often, in writing or editing books, or conducting workshops, I learn a lot from others—my collaborators on a book project or those who attend a workshop," Sid commented.

area of estate and tax planning for IRAs and other retirement savings accounts. But the way I present and teach comes from what I learned from Sid Kess.

Tax rules are hard to understand, even for CPAs. What I learned from Sid is that when you teach, you must speak so people understand you—not in tax code and not in legalese. That is why you learn so much at a Sid Kess program.

> *"...as a tax educator, you really need to be a translator of the tax code, just like Sid."*

I use that same approach when I present programs, and the results are remarkable. I love when people come to me and tell me that they finally understand something. That is because as a tax educator, you really need to be a translator of the tax code, just like Sid. You must also always include examples. I have found that examples are the absolute best learning tool, and I use them in all my articles, course manuals, and programs. I learned that from Sid as well.

My whole speaking style evolved from observing Sid and learning from him. I train our advisors and other presenters to make sure they speak so that people understand them. That's how you make an impression and get results.

Forget about taxes. Sid is a generous, caring person who finds a way to make everyone else feel like they matter. Thank you, Sid, for taking me under your wing, as you've done for so many others. I truly value and appreciate our friendship and association.

One thing that never changes is the feeling I still get when Sid Kess is on the phone. I know it will be something good!

* QTIP stands for *qualified terminable interest trust.* A QTIP trust is specially designed to provide for a surviving spouse but, at the same time, prevent the surviving spouse from changing beneficiaries.

---

1   Arthur J. Dixon, CPA, was managing partner of Oppenheim, Appel, Dixon and Co. He led the Tax department, which was renowned as a creative force in the field of securities taxation. See the New York State Society of CPAs website at www.nysscpa.org/trustedprof/archive/0503/1tp14a.htm.

Why Closer Collaboration Would Benefit Accountants and Lawyers

In Sid's opinion, accounting and legal professionals could collaborate more closely to their mutual benefit. For example, through their professional societies and other organizations, they could combine resources and efforts for specific purposes and get more value for their investment. Examples include joint sponsorship of conferences, workshops, and webinars of interest to both professions; publication of articles, reports, and books authored by CPAs and lawyers; and continuing professional education courses for both CPAs and lawyers. In addition, professional societies might host meetings that are open not just to CPAs or lawyers individually, but to professionals from both disciplines, or they might produce books and other publications and materials available not just to their own members but other professionals as well.

Sid Does Hollywood

In 1981, Sid and two lawyer colleagues flew from New York to Hollywood to record a video course featuring an update on the use of Form 1040, and based on a CPE course book. The video was to be broadcast across the United States via satellite. It was a pioneering effort in the development of continuing education for the home. The producers wanted Sid, the star of continuing education, for the recording, and they spared no expense to bring him and his colleagues to the West Coast.

Seated comfortably in first class, they tried to make use of the flight time to work on the book, which included a discussion of the Economic Recovery Tax Act of 1981, the law that reduced income tax rates and provided incentives for businesses, including changes in depreciation rates. It opened the door to

After collaborating with the California CPA Foundation on the document collection program, Sid was asked by several accounting associations to run a similar program for their members. "Within each association, I collected forms, checklists, client bulletins, and ran programs on how they could run a more profitable practice," Sid said. "The AICPA subsequently asked me to organize a program on Effectively Managing Your Tax Practice, where I collected forms from hundreds of firms and had the firms share their experiences." Today, professional organizations and tax publishers provide forms, checklists, and other documents to accounting professionals. "The AICPA, through its Tax Section and through the Personal Financial Planning Section and the Publications Division, currently makes available to the members outstanding practice aids. In addition, various publishers are sending out client letters and bulletins as well as checklists."

In another collaborative effort, Sid authored two books with Jim Cheeks: *The Kess Tax Planning Manual*, published by Warren Gorham & Lamont, and *A Practical Guide to Tax Planning*, published by Tax Management, Inc. Cheeks was an attorney and senior vice president of Thomson Reuters, previously known as RIA. "He had worked with me on my workshops, for more than 25 years," Sid said. "He was a close friend. I even moderated and helped arrange the memorial service for Jim at the Harvard Club this past May."

Some CPAs are accomplished writers. Others have unfulfilled potential as writers. Regardless, CPAs must have strong writing skills to communicate effectively with fellow practitioners, clients and others. Beyond satisfying professional needs, CPAs can apply their skills in writing for publication, an opportunity that practitioners sometimes overlook.

Writing

Sid's Tips on Writing for Publication

Today, there are more opportunities than ever for CPAs to write for publication. Part of the reason is the rapid growth of the online market, including websites, blogs, and e-newsletters. Some of these outlets are the products of traditional print media; others are exclusively digital media. Also, many media companies have trimmed staff because of the recession and other reasons, and they are looking for outside authors to contribute articles.

Sid offers these suggestions to CPAs who are just starting to write for publication, as well as experienced writers:

- *Know your market.* The sheer proliferation of media outlets means that you should pick your targets carefully. What print and online publications do you, and others in your organization, read? What do your clients read?

- *Know your audience.* First, decide which audience you want to reach. For example, your target audience may be small business owners, but

the widespread use of tax shelters in the United States.

They were under pressure to finish the book, which was not easy to do because of the complexities of the recently enacted 1981 tax act, and even more so because of the distraction in their first class cabin: famed producer Mel Brooks and legendary television sports announcer Howard Cosell. The two were enjoying themselves. Sid was trying to take advantage of the opportunity to talk with the superstars while also making some progress on the book. One of the lawyers, who was totally immersed in the book and oblivious to what was going on, didn't understand the accelerated depreciation rules and kept asking Sid to explain them. So there was Sid, schmoozing with the stars, working on the book, and trying to explain accelerated depreciation to the puzzled lawyer. Mention accelerated depreciation to him today and it probably brings back memories of that flight.

No visit to Los Angeles would be complete without a star sighting, and Sid and his team had theirs when they arrived at the hotel where they were staying. In the hotel lounge, they encountered Telly Savalas, the film and TV star best known for playing the title role in *Kojak*, the 1970s crime drama. Then, it was off to their room, where they worked all night to finish the book. The tired trio went to a studio lot in Hollywood the next morning, where they were to record the video. Sid was so exhausted that he asked to get a few minutes shut eye before the recording started. He was given a trailer where, he was told, the film star Angie Dickinson had slept on an earlier night. "Angie Dickinson and I slept in the same bed, but not at the same time," Sid said.

They recorded the program, and it was broadcast nationwide. However, the beaming of continuing education programs to homes was short lived, failing to attract enough viewers to keep it on the air. But it was a forerunner of today's widespread use of technology to deliver such programs to consumers.

For Sid, it was a memorable star turn in Hollywood.

which owners in this broad market do you want to reach? Second, determine which print or online publications, newsletters, and so forth are targeted to this audience. You can get an idea simply by reading these publications. Some also post editorial guidelines on their websites that define their markets. In any case, don't propose an article to an editor that will make it obvious that you don't know the publication's audience.

• *Think like a financial reporter.* While trying to come up with story ideas, read the current and back issues of your target publication to see what's already been written. Think like a reporter. Look for trends in the readers' industries and markets, such as changes in tax laws or regulations, and consider how these changes will affect them.

• *What are you proposing?* Do you want to write an article on a topic, or an opinion piece in which you air your views on an issue? Be clear in your own mind about what you are proposing.

• *Know how to approach a publication.* Editors are busy, and publishers usually have set rules about pitching stories to them. They usually want story proposals submitted by e-mail, or, less likely, in a letter, and they want short, succinct proposals. So, think about your proposal. Why are you proposing your article? What's the theme? Why should readers be interested?

• *Deliver on what you promise.* If you promise to deliver to an editor a 1,000 word article on the subject you've proposed by a certain date, deliver what you've promised. Before you submit the article, ask others in your organization to review it. (For that matter, you may be required to have others sign off before the article goes to the publication.) Check that the article is complete, accurate, provides useful information to readers, and offers suggestions on how they can apply that information in managing their businesses or careers, increasing their net worth, planning for retirement, or achieving other professional or personal goals. If the editor is happy with what you've written, you may be invited to contribute more articles in the future.

A final thought on writing: nurture the writing talent in your organization. If a CPA wrote for his or her high school or college newspaper, he or she may be able to assist with various writing projects, such as proposals, presentations, letters to clients, articles for the firm's website, and more.

How Sid Has Helped Others With Their Writing

The following are some examples of how Sid has assisted professionals in their writing and publishing pursuits.

"He is the Accountant's Rock Star"

Karen A. Notaro is portfolio managing editor for the Estate Planning Group at CCH, a WoltersKluwer business:

Sidney Kess has been a member of the CCH family since 1967, when he gave a seminar on the 1967 Act for our then sister company, Computax. Since that time, he has authored hundreds of books and continuing education materials, commented on tax legislation, provided guidance on trends in the marketplace, and helped launch several products that, today, form the basis of the Estate Planning Group.

Sid is a ready source of ideas and always offers suggestions for whom to contact for articles and other submissions. Without fail, the phrase "Sid Kess suggested I call" gets us past the administrative gate keeper and, invariably, we obtain that article or practitioner quote. No one has the respect and admiration of the industry like Sid does. He is the "accountant's rock star."

This was most evident to me several years ago, when we were going out for a group dinner with our advisory board, and a couple joined us in the hotel elevator along with Sid. When we left the hotel, the husband asked one of our party if that was Sid Kess on the elevator. We offered to introduce him to Sid. It turns out that the man had attended one of Sid's update seminars years before and, not only did Sid remember the seminar, he remembered the former student and the town in which he lived. We made the man's day when we took a picture of him and his wife with Sid. Passersby couldn't figure out who this angelic looking gentleman was and why people were clamoring to get their picture taken with him. It was a lot of fun watching people ask "Who is that?" as we were standing outside a Chicago hotel with a celebrity.

Professional, forthright, trustworthy, caring, kind, loyal, creative, innovative, teacher, and *mentor* are some of the words used to describe Sid, but the most important to me is *friend*. He is my mentor but, more importantly, he is my friend. I am truly honored to know him and to count him as a friend.

Thank you, Sid, for all that you have done for me, for CCH, and for the profession.

"Tax guru, idea man, marketing genius, mentor, friend"

Barbara Weltman is an attorney who has coauthored numerous CCH continuing professional education (CPE) programs with Sid, including the Audio Advisor, and is coeditor of the 2012 edition of the AICPA's Accountant's Business Manual.

Tax guru, idea man, marketing genius, mentor, friend. These are just a few of the titles that Sid Kess so justly deserves. In the 28 plus years that we've worked together, Sid has had a profound impact on my career and my personal life.

(continued on pg. 82)

(continued from pg. 81)

Professionally, we have worked together to develop new projects and ideas to help the accounting community. Many projects have been successful, others not, but all have reflected the highest quality of work. Bringing his enormous experience into play, he continually comes up with new ways to make information accessible and useful. His recall for tax details from years ago, when needed, is remarkable. He's taught me to be practical and to "do the best job in the time available."

He has also encouraged me to develop my own career. He's provided me with contacts, ideas, and opportunities to expand my horizons. I've been a speaker at the various programs that he's chaired. (I'm worn out after one session, but Sid energetically powers through all the sessions of the day.) Sid has cheered me along, shared my progress, and expressed pride when I've succeeded.

Personally, he's led by example to show me how best to handle people and put family first. He treats everyone fairly and with respect and can get along with even the most difficult of personalities. Everyone he deals with becomes a part of his "family," and he sincerely cares about how his family is doing. Bottom line: He is an indelible and invaluable part of my (and my family's) life; I'm privileged to work with him.

A life insurance broker started writing articles and books—and his business took off

Lee Slavutin graduated from medical school in 1974 in Australia, came to the United States in 1978, and practiced as a pathologist in New York until 1982. In 1983, he changed careers and entered the life insurance business. He is now a life insurance broker specializing in estate planning:

In the late 1980s, I was invited by an accountant in New York to speak at Sid's AICPA conference Tax Strategies for the High-Income Individual. That is how I met Sid.

We immediately had a good rapport and, several years later, Sid asked me to review his life insurance policies. We discovered that several policies were owned by Sid and realized that they should be assigned to an irrevocable insurance trust to exclude the proceeds from his estate. We completed the assignments.

Sid is a visionary. He saw how important this process was and how it could benefit CPAs and their clients. He said, "Lee, why don't you write an article and call it the *Life Insurance Policy Audit*?" I wrote the article for PPC's tax newsletter. That procedure has been a source of new business for me for over 20 years and, today, is a central part of my practice.

Then Sid saw something bigger. "Lee, why don't you write an article on insurance issues once a month for PPC and, in a few years, you will have enough material for a book?" I followed Sid's suggestion and, in 1998, the first edition of *A Guide to Life Insurance Strategies* was published by PPC. In 2011, the 12th edition was published by PPC/Thomson Reuters. I now update the book every year. It is a source of great satisfaction; it forces me to stay on top of new developments and is a great marketing tool.

Sid always taught me to keep things simple and practical and not to overwhelm the audience with technical details. He is a great model of how to communicate effectively.

But perhaps the greatest contributions from Sid Kess, for me and many other professionals, are his character and personality—he is a kind, generous, honest, gentle person, who continually encourages me to grow and learn. He asks for nothing in return. Sid and I often say that if I hired a marketing or PR firm for $1 million a year, I would never achieve the same results. Sid has also guided my son, who recently graduated from law school.

I am deeply indebted to Sid. And I am one of hundreds of thousands of professionals that Sid Kess has touched and empowered over the many years of his career.

Coauthor of a book with Sid

Arthur M. Seltzer is a Houston-based CPA:

Like many of my peers, I first became aware of Sid as a young accountant, reading some of his publications and listening to his audiotapes.

By 1981, I had joined a small local CPA firm as its tax partner and had the idea of developing a tax department as a profit center. I received an ad for a conference on tax department management that Sid was giving for the Pennsylvania CPA Society. I signed up to attend it and get feedback from Sid and the other attendees about some of the approaches I had developed. I brought with me some examples of the client publications I had written on specific tax topics.

At the conference Sid was particularly encouraging concerning the ideas I presented. My wife, who is not a CPA, sat in on the sessions and told me afterwards that she was impressed by his passion and empathy as well as his obvious competence.

Sid commended my writing and invited me to join his already substantial group of authors for his publications. At the time, our firm was just beginning to establish itself in the local market, and I reluctantly declined. I had occasional, but limited, contact with Sid over the years, but no significant contact until 2001, when the Missouri Society of CPAs invited me to speak at a conference that Sid would moderate. When I sent him the draft of my presentation on education planning, he responded enthusiastically and asked if I would agree to be interviewed for a book he was preparing, summarizing the approaches and recommendations of a number of practitioners to the changes contained in the 2001 tax reform act.[*] A number of my comments were quoted verbatim in the book, and some of my client publications and a substantial portion of the PowerPoint presentation I had prepared for the conference, were included in the appendix.

After the conference, Sid asked me to incorporate my ideas into a book, which has been published by the AICPA under both of our names. He subsequently had me revise the book for a video course, for which he interviewed me extensively on-camera and invited me to speak on the subject at one of his conferences.

We remain in contact from time to time, and he is always supporting and encouraging of my career.

---

[*] Economic Growth and Tax Relief Reconciliation Act of 2001.

Sid's ideas for a book's content and marketing

Julie A. Welch is a partner with Meara Welch Browne, PC, in Kansas City, Missouri:

Sid is truly an amazing individual. He does so much to help others. He is always giving everyone ideas and expects nothing in return.

In 1994, I coauthored the first edition of my book, *101 Tax Saving Ideas*. Imagine my surprise when I received an order for a dozen copies from Sid—and he didn't even know me! As a new author, that was a huge boost to my success and self-confidence. Since then, he has given me numerous ideas to incorporate into the book and even more ideas on how to market the book, since that is the hardest part.

For the past 10 years, I have served on Sid's planning committee for the AICPA's Tax Strategies for the High-Income Individual conference. Sid is so thoughtful on this committee. He listens to everyone's suggestions and tries to incorporate everyone's ideas. Meanwhile, he is constantly passing along ideas to better the conference, whether it is dealing more precisely with a topic, suggesting a new speaker for the program, or recommending innovative ways to market the conference.

Six years ago, when I was pregnant, I was asked to speak at one of Sid's conferences in New York. He called me before I traveled and made sure I had the contact information for the hospitals in case something happened. He called me again after I arrived at the hotel to make sure I traveled okay and to see if I needed anything.

In 2010, I was honored to be the committee member who presented Sid with the Sid Kess Award for Excellence in Teaching, yet upon receiving the award, he didn't even mention himself. Instead, he thanked all the committee members for their work and even the conference participants for attending.

Every time I talk with Sid, his first question is about how my two children are doing. Family is extremely important to Sid. He talks with his children every day.

Sid makes me feel like family when he bends over backwards to help or encourage me along with a project on which I am working. Even more important than a mentor, I consider Sid a very close friend and always cherish our phone calls and the times we get together.

How Sid helped an editor to improve a newsletter

G. Douglas Puckett is a CPA, CFP®, in Fort Worth, TX:

My first exposure to Sid Kess was as a participant in a CPE class he taught in the mid-1980s. At the time, he was probably the most well-known, widely respected speaker to CPAs and attorneys in America, having taught literally hundreds of thousands in his classes. Yet, his advice and comments were as practical and useful as those that might come from a trusted advisor sitting across the table, sharing a meal with you.

Several years later, that's exactly where I found myself. By then I was editing a tax update newsletter for a major publishing house, and Sid had joined our editorial board. We agreed to meet at least once a quarter wherever he was teaching at the time. It was during those working dinners that I developed not only a close business relationship with him but also a strong friendship. Each time we met, Sid came prepared with a stack of ideas of how we could make the newsletter more relevant and useful to its readers. He also provided specific suggestions on how to make it more profitable, including one that increased the paid circulation more than 30 percent in less than 90 days and another that produced a very technically proficient contributing author, who was a medical doctor by training. Only Sid would have the appropriate connections and business savvy to introduce me to an MD with specialized tax knowledge, who could write practical articles for the tax practitioner community.

As one of the nation's most prolific speakers, Sid's suggestions on how to present a topic and the importance of emphasizing the practical when teaching a class were valuable lessons for me as I started my own public speaking career. Through his connections, influence, and personal recommendations, he opened several doors of opportunity for speaking engagements—from major AICPA-sponsored conferences, to resort style CPE sessions across the globe—that likely wouldn't have otherwise been available to me.

All of this leads to one obvious conclusion: The key to understanding Sid is to know that he cares about those that he comes in contact with. He genuinely wants his students, friends, and business acquaintances to succeed. Over a more than 40 year career of teaching, writing, and advising, he has connected countless thousands of tax practitioners to new ideas and new opportunities to help them do just that.

People and Pets

Rachel Hirschfeld

Sid and I met many years ago in the beginning of my professional career. We have spoken almost every day since that day. I was giving a speech to the group from which Sid had just received the Hall of Fame Award for the National Association of Estate Planning Councils. The New York chapter presented the award to him at a local meeting. I was feeling insecure about giving my speech on the topic of financial planning for pets, but he encouraged me to continue speaking on the subject.

Sid suggested that accountants had the need for a book on protecting your pet and planning for their future in case anything should happen to the owner. Although I had never written a book, Sid encouraged me to contact the AICPA, who offered guidance, encouragement, contacts for reviewers, and persons for technical support. If not for Sid, I am not sure that I would

(continued on pg. 86)

(continued from pg. 85)

have completed the book *PETRIARCH: The Complete Guide to Financial and Legal Planning for a Pet's Continued Care*. Since then, he has advised me on a continuous basis about various other legal matters. I am one of hundreds that he watches over. He has a heart that is second to none. He tops the list of brilliance, humility, and concern for everyone he meets. He treats everyone with respect, from the bus driver who he compliments and thanks for stopping, to the leaders he meets in his daily walk. He is always there to support, guide, and encourage all alike. But this is not news to those who know him. Sid does this for everyone he has ever met. He helps so many people that it's almost unbelievable.

Ask CPAs about their skills, and a skill in media relations may not come to mind. But this is another area in which CPAs can develop their potential. The following is Sid's advice on how to build relationships with the media, and a look at his experience in working with reporters and writers over the years.

Media Relations

During his career, Sid developed strong professional relationships and personal friendships with reporters from the *New York Times*, the *Wall Street Journal*, and other publications. His ability to explain the complexities of changes in tax laws or regulations in simple, understandable terms was particularly valued. Here are a few of Sid's suggestions on working with the media:

- *Create a media list.* Develop a list of newspapers, television stations, and other media outlets in the city where your office is located, which would be considered your "home market." In time, you can expand your list to include professional journals, trade publications, national newspapers, and other media. You can get contact information directly from the media and from various print and online directories.

- *Develop relationships.* You can start by contacting and developing relationships with reporters and editors in your home market. Think of story ideas that might be of interest to reporters, for example, what tax issues their readers should be concerned about.

- *Issue press releases.* You can write press releases on topics of interest to the media and their readers, such as tax planning tips, estate planning suggestions, advice on managing business, or personal spending. You can send your releases directly to the media in your local market, to trade publications and professional journals, and other media outlets. You can also use various services to distribute releases, for example, if you want to issue a release nationally or put out a release targeted to a particular market segment.

- *Create a website or start a blog.* You can create a website that includes information about your company, its executives, the services it offers, press releases you've issued, and so forth. You also can create a blog that provides viewers with news of interest, your comments and observations on issues, and other content. But you must be prepared to invest time, thought, and resources in creating a website and writing a blog that keeps attracting viewers, including current or prospective clients. Before you commit, you might talk to business associates and others about their experience with websites.

- *Establish a reputation as a reliable, trustworthy source.* Reporters want sources who are available (today, not a day or three days from now), knowledgeable, and, most important, trustworthy. It takes time to develop relationships with reporters. But as Sid has proven in his career, those relationships can endure for years once the bond is established. He never asked for anything from them in return. "I just tried to be helpful, and if I didn't know the answer to a question, I would suggest other sources. I didn't want to say something that might not have been accurate and put the writer in the position of publishing inaccuracies."

As with managing your business, you should have a plan for your practice development. What are your goals? How will you realize them? This can be a simple plan, carried out in incremental steps, for example, spending an hour a week on preparing a speech or writing an article. The important part is to have a plan.

The following are some examples of how Sid has assisted media relations professionals in their work:

Sidney Kess: Tax Guru and Friend

Robert Metz is a former Market Place Columnist for the New York Times:

When I was an aspiring newsman at the *New York Times*, we "copy boys" faced a seven-year apprenticeship that had Columbia Journalism and other master's prepared graduates filling paste pots, running errands, and doing every other first-step-on-the-ladder chore a "gofer" is expected to do.

Wonder of wonders, the *Times* needed a tax columnist and, as an economics major with a law degree tucked into my jeans, I was chosen for the task. Thus, I became a columnist before I began as a reporter, which I believe was unheard of then.

Obviously, I was underwater. Sensing the complexity of the subject matter and indulging my ambition to write human interest stories while eager to move up in the organization, I accepted the post with mixed feelings. After all, I had dismissed all tax courses in college and in law school as, well, boring.

(continued on pg. 88)

(continued from pg. 87)

What did I know about taxes? Fortunately, and early on, I met Sidney Kess. This was, as Sidney reminds me, nearly half a century ago. I don't remember where we met, but I do remember Sidney as a manager in a Big 8 firm, who could spit out answers to any question that came up on the tax law. On deadline, such a source is priceless to a reporter.

The first time we met, he was toting Library of Congress sized folders along with his luggage, looking to the entire world like a suave, overworked porter in Penn Station.

Fortunately, as the years passed, computers kicked in, and Sidney was able to jettison the "dead tree library" for a word processor that lightened his load enormously.

When Sidney and I got together, he always seemed soft-spoken and even self-effacing. I hadn't seen him in action.

But one day, the financial editor of the *Times* asked me to meet with the members of his church, and Sidney volunteered to come with me. I was still out of my depth. Someone asked a question, I looked at Sidney, and suddenly "The Quiet Man" became a locomotive of tax ignorance destruction. He projected with great panache and was the star of the evening.

My key work with Sidney at the *Times* was to prepare two full pages of tax advice copy that appeared in the paper days before the April 15 tax filing deadline. Sidney and I worked together on this project year after year. We even worked together on a tax guide published by a top book publisher for several years.

If I haven't made it clear by now, you can guess that Sidney was, by far, my best source on tax matters and, not to understate the obvious to those who know him, he became a lifelong friend. He has always given of himself more than was expected when asked to help. He is, as they say, a *mensch*.

How Sid helped a *New York Times* writer get her career rolling

Deborah Rankin is a former financial writer for the New York Times:

Sid helped me get my career rolling when I joined the *New York Times* as a financial writer in the late 1970s. My beat was taxes and accounting, subjects I was only superficially acquainted with after a Knight Bagehot* mid-career sabbatical at Columbia University.

The *Times* suggested that I contact Sid for guidance, and he immediately took me under his wing. He introduced me to savvy and helpful CPAs and tax lawyers and gave me a crash course in the big issues of the day.

---

*   Knight-Bagehot Fellowship Program in Economics and Business Journalism, Columbia University.

Sid was my greatest resource of all. He was patient beyond belief and tutored me in the fine points of individual and corporate taxes. Together, we launched a multipart series on individual taxes for the *Times* that was later reprinted in booklet form for many years after.

He was as concerned as I was with the accuracy of the series and would call me at odd times while he was on the road for the AICPA. When the phone rang at 6:30 a.m., I always knew who was on the other line.

Sid never expected or asked for anything in return—just that the *Times* convey the latest information in the most accurate and reader-friendly form possible. I was honored to be admitted to Sid's circle of friends and am truly touched that he thought to include me among the many people who are writing tributes to him for this book. I was, and am, very lucky to have made Sid's acquaintance. He is a real *mensch*.

"He is without doubt the doyen of the tax practitioner community"

Jan Rosen currently is a financial writer for the New York Times. *She is writing here as an individual and not for, or on behalf of, the* Times:

Sid Kess is remarkable—professionally, personally, indeed, in every way. He is, without doubt, the doyen of the tax practitioner community. His knowledge of tax law is encyclopedic; more importantly, he knows how to apply it to people in particular situations not just to the rich and people engaged in complex business and investing strategies, but also people who are poor and struggling, like a waitress in a coffee shop. Most of us might have tipped her $1. After chatting with her, Sid volunteered to prepare a tax return claiming credits that she had not known existed.

The encounter with the waitress was a single but telling event. Sid loves people, all sorts and conditions of people, and spends a great deal of time helping people, both personally and through charitable activities, often volunteering and leading conferences for the UJA-Federation of New York.

Sid has also helped me many times, functioning essentially as a personal tutor in individual income tax law. I am a journalist and joined the staff of the *New York Times* more than 40 years ago. Among my assignments at the *Times* have been numerous pieces on taxes and personal finance. Long ago, I wrote two columns, *Your Money* and *Tax Watch*, and Sid was, without doubt, my number one source. I must stress that I am writing this as an individual, not for, or on behalf of, the *Times*; although, I know that Sid has been equally helpful to many others at the paper over the years when they, too, were working on tax articles.

What is remarkable about Sid is not only his extensive and up-to-date knowledge of the subject but also his willingness, even eagerness, to put writers in contact with others in his tremendous network of experts, many of whom I have met at AICPA conferences he has led. Many professionals are pleased to be quoted in articles because readers may infer that they are leading experts, but Sid is unique, in my experience, in wishing to put writers in contact with others in his field.

(continued on pg. 90)

(continued from pg. 89)

In addition, he often offers to work with writers after the initial interview to double-check both facts and wording. Tax law is complex, and sometimes there are conflicting precedents when different courts have decided seemingly similar cases. Sometimes a word like *generally* will suffice, but not always, and Sid is invaluable in sniffing out potential problems and getting the wording just right.

Such behind-the-scenes efforts do not show up in print or win a following among readers, but they are the beneficiaries of Sid's patience and dedication to his profession. And, if I, as a journalist, have helped make our nation's complex tax code a bit more accessible to readers, it is due in no small part to Sid Kess, a wonderful human being, as I am sure his thousands of friends across the country will attest.

"My most memorable day with Sid was Sept. 11, 2001."

R. Thomas Herman was with the Wall Street Journal *from 1968–2009 and was author of the Tax Report from 1993–2009:*

For more than three decades, Sid Kess has been a marvelous friend and cherished mentor. He cares deeply about his family and friends, and he has never been too busy to help on a story.

I met Sid through Blanche Etra, the mother of my college roommate, Don Etra, at a conference in New York several decades ago. Since then, I have attended many conferences run by Sid and long have marveled at his rare ability to make tax stories and concepts both clear and interesting. He has a delightful sense of humor and a keen sense of irony.

My most memorable day with Sid was September 11, 2001.

That morning, at around 8:30, I arrived at my desk at the *Wall Street Journal*, which then was at 200 Liberty Street, across the highway from the twin towers of the World Trade Center. I began rewriting and polishing a speech I was scheduled to give that day at noon at a conference run by Sid at the Marriott Marquis Hotel near Times Square.

Just as I was finishing the speech, I heard a tremendous explosion. I thought the large window behind me might shatter. I leaped out of my chair, looked out the window, and saw the horror of the top floors of the north tower of the World Trade Center in flames.

We were told there was no need to evacuate the building. A television station reported that it was probably an accident. A plane had flown into the north tower. I called my wife, who was at our home across the street in Gateway Plaza, and told her we should get ready to leave soon for the Marriott Marquis.

About 15 minutes later came another explosion. Flames shot out of the south tower. At this point, I didn't wait for an announcement. I threw the text of my speech into a bag along with a few other items, headed for the exits, walked downstairs, and ran across the street. My wife and I walked briskly uptown. We were a few blocks away when we felt the earth rumble as the south tower went down. We ran and were able to escape the debris storm created by the tower's collapse. Later, we watched the second tower go down.

We walked several miles to the Marriott Marquis, where we saw Sid and also my college roommate, Don Etra, who lives in Los Angeles, but was in town that day. Their calmness and coolness were reassuring. To my surprise, however, Sid told me that the tax conference was continuing. (Mayor Giuliani asked everyone to stay put as all transportation had been suspended and, aside from those participants who had rushed to the hospital to donate blood, the program went ahead.) Several hundred people were still there, and Sid said he expected me to speak as scheduled during the lunch program. I retreated to the bathroom, where I burst into tears as the full impact of what my wife and I had witnessed sank in. I also began feverishly reworking the speech I had prepared.

When I got to the podium, Sid presented me with The Sidney Kess/UJA-Federation of New York Award for Excellence in Financial Reporting in the Field of Taxation. He shook my hand and gave me a hug.

I felt another wave of emotion coming up from deep within. I quickly reached for a large glass of water, swallowed it quickly, and asked everyone for a moment of silence to remember the thousands of people who had been murdered that morning before my very eyes. That gave me more time to recover.

I can't remember what I said on that tragic day, but the words on the top of the award Sid gave me speak volumes about Sid and why I feel so honored to know him and to call him a close friend: *Without understanding, there is no knowledge; without knowledge, there is no understanding.*

5

Find and Connect
With People

A host of professionals have received a call
from Sid or had an encounter with Sid that
opened up unexpected opportunities: public
speaking and teaching, exposure to audiences
of current and potential clients, business leads,
writing articles and books, networking and
more. He urges CPAs and other professionals
to reach out to other professionals to provide
advice and assistance and offer guidance
and support. In doing so, CPAs not only are
helping others, they also are building and
strengthening relationships and networks,
giving back to the profession, and, sometimes,
finding opportunities, for example, volunteer
work for a not-for-profit organization can result
in connecting with people who are potential
clients. Connecting with people is mutually
beneficial, those who are helped could in turn
help the helpers. For example, a CPA who has

> **Leaving a mark on the world**
>
> John Connors is president of the Tax Educators' Network in Mequon, Wisconsin.
>
> Probably the most important and impressive lesson that I've learned from Sid is that there are individuals who are truly not looking out for themselves. Not only on a professional level, but also on a personal one, Sid has sought to help me in whatever way he can since the first time that I met him. He has recommended me numerous times for teaching opportunities and other professional endeavors.
>
> But more valuable have been his kind and guiding words of advice regarding his experiences as a single parent and the unconditional love that he always showed his children. I can only hope that I can someday leave even a small mark on our world in the same fashion that Sid has done.

recommended a practitioner for a job may later be helped by the practitioner with the search for a new job.

One area in which CPAs can help the profession is in finding talented CPE teachers.

Talent Hunter

Sid has not only been a teacher (see chapter 2) but also a talent hunter, recruiting talented people to speak at his workshops and conferences. He often has formed lasting friendships with people he recruits, mentoring and supporting them in their careers and in their growth as professionals and people.

Talent hunting doesn't stop with Sid. The professionals he has recruited for his workshops, conferences, and other programs can themselves become talent hunters and, in the process, add to the pool of highly talented teachers that are in increasing demand in the profession.

Where do you look for talent?

• *Start in your own market*. You may see teachers that excel in their subject, possess strong presentation skills, and provide information of practical value at places such as meetings of state CPA societies, state continuing professional education (CPE) classes, and other state or local meetings and events.

• *Look at meetings of other professionals*. Although your focus is on recruiting CPAs, you can look for other talented professionals to recruit, for example, if you happen to attend a meeting of a lawyer's group.

• *Ask others*. Ask your professional colleagues, friends, and acquaintances if they know of talented, but undiscovered, teachers.

• *Ask your audience*. "I have often asked people in my audience to recommend a CPA or other professional who is extremely knowledgeable about a subject area and a polished speaker," Sid said.

• *Attend workshops outside accounting*. Sid recruited Blanche Lark Christerson, managing director at Deutsche Bank Private Wealth Management in New York (see page 100) after hearing her speak at a Deutsche Bank program on estate planning.

• *Talk to others who conduct workshops*. Sid has recruited speakers from CPAs and others who have gone into the business of conducting their own workshops.

When you do find talented teachers, you might suggest to them that they contact a local or state CPA society and offer to present a program. These organizations often are looking for program ideas and presenters. Starting at the local level helps a teacher gain experience and decide whether he or she wants to move to a bigger platform. Once he or she gains local experience, he or she might apply to the AICPA to participate in its workshops. The AICPA also provides training for members who speak at its workshops.

Sid once got a call from an executive who conducted tax workshops at the AICPA. A speaker on venture capital had canceled his speaking engagement at an upcoming workshop. Could Sid suggest a replacement? He could because he knew someone who practiced not only as a CPA but also as an attorney and venture capital specialist and was interested in speaking at AICPA programs.

The following are some examples of how Sid has personally helped CPAs, attorneys, and other professionals with their careers as CPE teachers:

"World champion opportunity giver"

Steve Siegel, JD, LL.M., is the president of Morristown, NJ-based The Siegel Group:

One of the most important things a person can give another is opportunity—and Sid is the world champion opportunity-giver. Time and again, he has recommended people he cares about to others who have speaking, writing, and work opportunities. Sid never asks for anything in return—only the expectation that you will do a good job. He is always the first person to call after a program to compliment the participants on the job done and express his pleasure over how much the attendees benefitted from the presentations.

Sid first reached out to me to speak at the UJA-Federation of New York Conference he organizes in New York City every year. He had read some of the materials I had written for a legal publication and wanted to get me involved. From that modest beginning, he referred me to a number of his colleagues. Since then, I can trace a trail of opportunities that have allowed me to speak for a wide variety of organizations in numerous venues across the country, to present webinars, and to write books and articles for prestigious publications. This trail always can be traced back to something Sid did—a good word here, a recommendation there.

When you spend time with Sid away from the meeting rooms, you have to expect a lot of interruptions from the phone calls he gets. He speaks to his children and grandchildren on a daily basis. They obviously appreciate his warmth and wisdom, as do those of us who have come to know him on a professional basis.

Sid's generosity of opportunity is not just limited to a few lucky individuals. There are many of us all over the country that have been touched by him—we are all proud to call ourselves part of the "Sid Kess Tax Team." If all of us do what we can to offer others opportunities, maybe together we can approach, but probably never equal, what Sid, as one very special and generous person, has done for us.

"What really matters is how much Sid cares about people"

Martin S. Finn, is founding partner of Lavelle & Finn, LLP in Latham, NY:

Although I had known of Sid Kess for many years through his work with various organizations educating tax practitioners, including the AICPA, I had not had the pleasure of meeting him personally until 2002, when I first presented at the AICPA Tax Strategies for the High-Income Individual conference. I recall fondly Sid introducing himself to me and making me feel so welcome as part of the conference faculty—a valuable member of the group.

I have been a presenter at that conference ever since. In 2008, I joined the conference steering committee, which Sid chairs, and which plans the conference each year. It is as a member of that conference committee that I have gotten to know Sid even better and grown to consider him a dear friend.

Sid has a vast and incredible knowledge of the tax law, and he can convey that knowledge effortlessly and in an incredibly understandable manner to an audience. What really matters is how much Sid cares about people.

Sid cares about his audience. He consistently stresses to his conference faculty, "Give them something they can take back to their office and talk to their clients about. Give them tips they can use right away to generate revenue. Do this, and they will keep coming back." And he's right. He has been a great educator through the years primarily because he understands—and cares about—his audience.

He also cares about his faculty and colleagues. Whenever I speak to Sid, whether we are together at a conference or on the phone, he asks me about my family—and he listens to my answers. And he remembers. In subsequent conversations, he'll ask how my "college" son is doing or if my "golfing" son can still beat me on the course. When I have had the opportunity to bring my wife or one of my sons with me to a conference, Sid will engage them in conversation and always tell them what a terrific and bright husband/dad they have. Now, they don't necessarily believe him, but I like hearing it.

Sid is a mentor. In our years together, he has taught me how to be a more engaging presenter and a better educator. He has shown me how to be a more valuable planning committee member. He has demonstrated what it takes to put together a high level conference and to get the best performance from a faculty.

Why no one else volunteered for this workshop

Albert Grasso is the former president of Chuhak & Tecson, a Chicago law firm, and now of counsel with the firm. He presented at a Sid workshop in Casper, Wyoming, in December 1978. No one else had volunteered. The fact that the temperature was around zero degrees Fahrenheit may have had something to do with it.

By 1984, Grasso and Andy R. Biebl, CPA, were assisting Sid with producing video programs for both the Corporate and Individual Income Tax Workshops. "At the time, I had a mustache and a full beard. Sid joked that I had more hair on the bottom of my head than both he and Andy combined had on the tops of their heads."

In 1992, Andy and I decided to bring our then teenage daughters to New York during the taping of one of the video programs. Sid insisted that we all go out to dinner. Sid regaled our daughters with stories of tax adventures and misadventures—some to my personal embarrassment. To this day, my daughter speaks fondly of both the trip to New York and Sid.

Getting on the national scene

Andrew Biebl, CPA, is a principal with LarsonAllen LLP and heads the firm's federal tax services group:

Sid was responsible for getting me on the national scene as an AICPA speaker and in mentoring me, and many others, in our careers as discussion leaders for CPE. Sid taught us the importance not only of teaching what had changed but also on the opportunities and defensive strategies to assist the practitioner in carrying the development to their client. Sid was famous for his "tips and traps" questions and in prompting us to deliver a higher level of learning to our CPA colleagues.

Not only was Sid a great professional mentor to so many of us, but he continues to be a kind and caring individual who took the time to know our families. He would often call solely for the reason of checking on how our speaking careers were going and how our family was doing. I recall many speaking trips to New York to work on videos with Sid when he went out of his way to extend kindnesses to my children and accommodate our visit.

The entire profession owes a debt of gratitude to Sid for his leadership in not only conducting training, but for inspiring many others to follow in his footsteps as providers of education to the profession.

"Secret mentor"

David De Jong, LL.M., CPA, is a principal with Stein Sperling Bennett De Jong Driscoll PC, in Rockville, Maryland:

When I came out of law school in 1975, I was hired by the tax department of a mid-sized company, despite having taken only two courses in law school. I was told that the best way to keep up on tax developments was to listen to Sid Kess' monthly tapes of new developments. I dutifully listened to them in my car for several years as I obtained my master of laws in taxation degree and my CPA certificate.

I was honored in the late 1980s when I was asked to teach a number of Sid's two-day corporate and individual tax programs, which he put together for the AICPA. In the ensuing two decades, I have been proud to speak at a number of his conferences, to serve on panels that he moderated, and to be a participant on several video tapes of new tax legislation for the AICPA.

Little did I know when I first started listening to Sid's tapes in 1975 that I would be one of his speakers and panelists. Little did he know that he was a secret mentor to me from the first cassette tape, when I heard his brilliant mind and distinguished voice summarize the month's individual and business tax developments.

Today, I make 15–20 speeches a year, in which I update recent tax developments. I often think back to the education that I received from Sid and reflect on how much I enjoy, as he does, the passing of knowledge to both contemporaries and the next generation of scholars.

"Sid's passion for quality CPE is evident"

Kurt Oestriecher is a CPA with Oestriecher & Company, CPAs in Alexandria, Louisiana:

I was first introduced to Sid by my father, Emile Oestriecher, CPA. As a small firm tax practitioner, my father relied heavily on the annual updates Sid presented in Louisiana, and we went to one of his classes early in my career.

It did not take long during that class to understand why my father and other Louisiana CPAs had such a high regard for Sid. I was amazed at what I learned that day and the ease with which Sid discussed complex topics. It was a significant day for me in my career. I had no idea at that time that I would ever teach a CPE course, but once I started, I used that day as a template for how I should conduct my courses.

My father told me how prepared Sid was for his courses and how he had an uncanny ability to translate complex tax subjects into words understandable to those of us who do not study the tax code and new tax laws on a daily basis.

I began teaching CPE courses for the AICPA in 1998 and was fortunate enough to spend some time with Sid at an instructor forum hosted by the AICPA in May, 2000. His passion for quality CPE was, and still is, evident.

Sid taught me that the 8 hours of CPE earned should be the least significant part of the day. Any instructor can discuss a topic for 400 minutes, and all the participants would receive their CPE credit.

"I hope to help another tax professional like Sid helped me"

Carolyn R. Turnbull is director of tax in the Atlanta office of Moore Stephens Tiller LLC:

I first met Sid in the mid-1990s, when I was asked to perform the technical review for the AICPA's Corporate Tax Return video course. I had been in public accounting approximately 10 years at the time. Since that time, I have worked with Sid on several continuing professional education courses, and I continue to work with Sid today as a presenter for the Corporate Tax Returns video course, as well as a member of the steering committee for the AICPA Tax Strategies for the High-Income Individual conference.

Sid has been one of the best mentors and role models that anyone could ask for. Because of him, I have been given the opportunity to speak to hundreds of CPAs and attorneys at various conferences and continuing professional education seminars across the United States. Sid has also expanded my networking opportunities by introducing me to other tax professionals he has worked with.

Sid is always willing to listen and to share his knowledge. I strive to model my professional life after Sidney Kess. My goal is to someday be able to help another tax professional the way that Sid has helped me.

Heeding the call

Jeremiah W. Doyle is senior vice president at BNY Mellon Wealth Management in Boston:

A number of years ago, I received a voicemail from Sid Kess, asking me to call him. While I did not know Sid personally at the time, I knew him from books he had written that I used when I was in college and law school 30 years ago. At first I thought it was a wrong number—I couldn't imagine why Sid was calling *me*.

I returned the call, and Sid asked me to speak at one of his programs in New York City. My topic was the income taxation of trusts and estates. I immediately accepted. I thought my encounter would be a one-time event. Quite the contrary. Sid has been a colleague, a mentor, a sounding board, but most importantly, a friend. Sid has devoted countless hours to making sure CPAs receive the most up-to-date, useful, and practical information needed for their practices.

I have never met a person so willing to help the accounting and legal professions.

"Sid Kess Tax Team"

Blanche Lark Christerson is managing director at Deutsche Bank Private Wealth Management in New York:

I first met Sid when he hustled up to me after a speech I gave at a Deutsche Bank event many years ago. He told me I had done a 'beauty-ful' job and wanted to have me on one of the programs he was putting together for the AICPA. The rest, as they say, is history.

I have now spoken at countless programs that Sid has put together and love being part of the "Sid Kess Tax Team." I have greatly benefitted from Sid's shrewd insights on how best to present things and what really matters to an audience. I treasure Sid's mantra to us speakers: "Be practical. Give them something they can start using right away in their practice." It's great advice in so many ways.

Sid is a true impresario, both in the programs he creates, and the difference he makes in people's lives. He not only finds the best speakers for the most topical subjects, he selflessly promotes people's careers.

CPAs can find and connect not only with fellow professionals but also with people in the community, for example, by teaching courses on financial literacy at a local high school or college, or mentoring students majoring in accounting or other subjects. Or maybe, as Sid has done, simply saying hello to a stranger.

How to Give Back

Every CPA—indeed everyone—can give back in ways large or small. A few suggestions from Sid follow:

- *Get started.* Whether you are a student or a practitioner, put in the time and effort to give back to the profession, the community, and your family and friends. It could be an hour a week of volunteer time or five hours a week, whatever you can spend.

- *The profession.* Volunteer to teach a program for CPAs and other professionals. Join a committee of a state society or the AICPA. Offer to assist with a research project. Mentor an accounting student or young professional just starting a career in accounting.

- *The community.* Teach a course on financial literacy to high school or community college students. Assist a local legal aid society that needs accounting expertise. Find an unmet need in the community, and think of a way to meet it. Organize, plan, and put your idea into action. Consider starting a program to provide math tutoring to students or workers who need to improve their math skills to qualify for a job. It's an opportunity to develop leadership skills.

- *Family*. Spend time with family and friends, talking, listening, relaxing, and doing activities. Offer to help with a job search, career guidance, homework, transportation, getting medical care, or other needs.

- *Start your own organization*. For example, start a group that might interest young people in becoming CPAs. One model for this is Career Opportunities in the Accounting Profession (COAP). Sponsored by the New York State Society of CPAs, COAP educates minority high school students on the many facets of the accounting profession and builds skills to help them succeed in college and the business world.

> ## Why Would Sid Bring Four or Five Suitcases on a Two-Day Trip?
>
> The first time J. Paul Stockwell met Sid was in 1974, when he had just started his CPA practice in Jackson, Mississippi. Stockwell was on a CPA continuing education committee that had invited Sid to visit. Stockwell called him beforehand and said he would pick up Sid at the airport. He asked Sid how much luggage he would be bringing. Sid said four or five bags. "Why would he need to bring that much luggage from New York for a two-day visit here?" Stockwell thought. As he discovered when Sid arrived, Sid would be on the road for many days and nights traveling the country, and Jackson was one of many stops.

More than 2,700 students have taken part in COAP programs at 10 different universities since it began in New York State in 1987.[1]

- *Mentoring*. When he was riding a crowded bus in New York one day, Sid struck up a conversation with a fellow passenger, a middle-aged black man who had come into the city to take a high school equivalency test. The man regretted that when he was young, he hadn't had an adult in his life to guide and mentor him. The encounter reinforced for Sid what he already knew: that there is a great need for mentors in society. CPAs can help by mentoring high school or college students who aspire to careers in accounting or other fields; veterans who have returned home from Iraq and Afghanistan and have enrolled in school; adults who are trying to improve their reading skills; or help with financial literacy programs sponsored by the AICPA or other organizations.

The following are just some of the ways in which Sid has personally given back:

---

1   "Adelphi COAP Program Encouraging Minority Students," press release, New York State Society of CPAs, June 22, 2011, www.nysscpa.org/page/adelphi-coap-program-encouraging-minority-students.

"It is hard to imagine anyone who gives more to the profession"

Martin Shenkman, CPA, PFS, JD, is an estate planner in Paramus, NJ:

"Sid Kess is a very special person. Before I knew Sid personally, he was that ubiquitous author whose name appeared on more tax seminars, articles, books, and other resources than anyone. It was almost hard to fathom that 'Sid Kess' was a person rather than a company with a horde of writers.

"One day, out of the blue (way out of the blue!) I received a phone call from a man who identified himself as Sid Kess. Immediately I was trying to figure out which colleague was playing a prank. Sid explained that he had been following my career, was very proud of my accomplishments, and wanted to help me get more involved in the AICPA. I remember the day, where I was sitting, and all the details of the call.

"From that off the charts phone call many years ago, I have had the good fortune to work with Sid on many AICPA and charitable programs and projects. I've learned that Sid has reached out to many people, practitioners, charities, and causes and touched many lives. Sid has become, if it is not too presumptuous to say, a friend and personal mentor.

"While the almost endless well of technical materials Sid has produced would inspire anyone, educate any tax professional, and more, what truly sets Sid apart is not his technical brilliance or his myriad of accomplishments, but his compassion, volunteerism, concern for others, integrity.

"At the pinnacle of the profession Sid can manage to have a warm and personal word for scores, perhaps hundreds of attendees at a program. He remembers names, personal issues, and so much more. When he greets someone, he asks how they are, not in the superficial way that so many in our busy and hectic world ask, but because he truly cares. It is hard to imagine anyone who gives more to the profession, to charity, and to every individual he touches.

"The Jewish holiday of Chanukah represents the universal message of freedom, hope, and light that is common to all. The symbol of these universal aspirations is the Menorah, a candelabrum holding 8 candles, one for each day of the holiday, and another candle used to light them. A number of years ago on the holiday of Chanukah, I gave Sid a Menorah as a gift that contained the following engraving: "To Sid Kess who has brought so much light into so many lives." And truly he has, and continues to do so.

Sid Kess gives of his time and his heart like no other. It has been an honor and inspiration to know him and work with him. The lessons learned from Sid help me keep focus on what is really important: professional integrity, competency, and giving back to the profession, charities, and individuals whenever called upon, not when it might be practical or convenient. Sid has truly made the world a little kinder and, hopefully, all of us who have been touched by Sid will continue and grow that legacy.

"Super Giver"

Perry A. Shulman is a CPA based in East Rockaway, New York:

In Bob Burg's and John David Mann's 2007 business coaching book, "The Go–Giver,"* the authors offered these concepts: Personal wealth and success is the by-product of making the world a better place, and the more successful a person is, the more they are willing to share their secrets with others.

The superstars see the world differently than most. The successful view the world as a place of inexhaustible treasures rather than as a place of limitations.

Sid is a superstar and a super giver. He takes an interest in his many professional colleagues and students, often inquiring about what their challenges are and then suggesting courses of action to help them succeed. In many instances, he suggests that they call another colleague of his, who may be one of the foremost experts in the country in a particular technical field, and "tell them that you are a personal friend of Sid's. They will help you with your quandary."

Not only does Sid extend himself to his many thousands of students but even to the facilities staff at Rockefeller Center in New York, where his offices are located. He takes a personal interest in the elevator operators, security guards, and maintenance people, knowing many by name, as well as their children's names, vacation plans, and personal challenges.

My association with Sid began over 20 years ago, when I attended Sid's two-day Individual Income Tax Workshop in White Plains, NY. It was given on a Sunday and Monday, specifically to accommodate students who observed the Sabbath. At lunch, he specifically sat at the "kosher food table" and conversed with the participants. He inquired about where they worked and if their religious observances hindered their advancement at their respective firms. In those days, although many of the New York firms were managed by Jewish accountants, there was a tremendous discrimination directed at Sabbath observers, and Sid would help anyone he could.

Larry King was once asked if his superstar guests are as genuinely nice as they seem on television. He responded "the bigger they are, the nicer they are." Sid is a superstar with a heart of gold. There is nothing in the world that he would not do for his friends, colleagues, and students.

---

* Bob Burg and John David Mann, *The Go-Giver: A Little Story About a Powerful Business Idea*, New York: Portfolio Hardcover, 2007.

A "Giant" in the profession helps a "kid"

David M. Spitzberg is a Philadelphia-based CPA:

In November 1976, with minimal experience not only in the professional but also in the practical worlds, I had just begun working for a single-owner CPA firm. My employer sent me to Sid's Individual Income Tax Returns Workshop to start to learn. So off I went to the workshop in a large Philadelphia hotel ballroom packed with professionals to begin to understand the basics. Sid's approach was sensible. He taught us a concept. We then read questions, and he explained the answers. Everything was done in practical, uncomplicated English. The class binder was a great organized reference with explanations, examples, questions, answers, and practice checklists. Sid also provided useful suggestions to help us make money.

I continued to attend the annual program. Two years after finishing one of the programs, I had a question about the printed materials. I called Sid's office in New York City and was told that he was teaching in San Francisco. Guess what? He actually called me back that afternoon. I just couldn't believe it. Here's a giant in the profession calling a kid to help him out! That's when I knew that I had a very special friend.

And I was right. Sid continues to prove that the "greatest" can also be the nicest. I recall him always asking about my family and my practice after each year's class. Since that special phone call, he has always invited me to sit with him during lunch, whenever possible. Just imagine the people that I have had an opportunity to meet. I actually met a gentleman who later sold his practice to me. We often remember the time when I told Sid that I couldn't take him to the train station because my wife was expecting. My daughter, now 27, was born that evening. Before my son's graduation from college, Sid invited my son and me to meet him in New York City. Sid provided him with sensible and encouraging advice.

Sid has taught me the power of continuing to learn. He continues to guide me when I need technical help. I rely upon Sid for his wisdom in making sometimes difficult decisions about clients. My practice has been greatly enhanced by learning to be proactive. He has encouraged me to write articles and speak before groups and the media. And yes, Sid taught me to be practical in my approach—to speak and write in clear, brief, uncomplicated English. I've received many honors as a result of following Sid's guidance.

I continue to be very fortunate, to say the least, to call Sidney Kess my dear friend. We consider ourselves family. How many people have the opportunity during their lives to be so enriched?

All in the family

Mariette O'Malley, CPA, JD (Tax), CFP® is a partner with O'Malley and O'Malley LLP, Cinnaminson, NJ:

I don't recall the first time I heard the name Sid Kess. I know I wasn't in high school when Dad (Charles K. O'Malley, managing partner, O'Malley and O'Malley) introduced my siblings and me to Sid's "cast of characters"—daughter Debbie,

Sylvia the piano teacher, and all the rest over our dinner table. Sid and his annual tax review in Philadelphia had become a part of our after Thanksgiving family tradition.

Over the years, my dad and my brother, Chuck, a LaSalle grad and second generation accountant, made the annual trek to Sidney Kess' Corporate & Individual Tax Workshops the weekend after Thanksgiving. My mom, Kathy, a public accountant, joined him a few years later at the workshops, and Sidney began to learn the details of our family. With six children, there was a lot to learn, but Sid absorbed the details of our lives as if we were his own, and so we would become.

I attended my first "Sid conference" during my senior year at LaSalle College. Dad thought it would be "a good experience." Like any child, I was dreading the good experience, but I was in for a life-changing surprise. This ball of energy popped up on the stage by 7:30 a.m., checking mikes, pulling out reference volumes, strategically setting up water glasses and tea cups. Class started promptly at 8:00 a.m., and the schedule for the day was set out. It was the first of many lessons I would learn from Sid.

Over the years, my parents had become somewhat friendly with Sid (who wasn't?), offering him rides to the train or inviting him to dinner when we stayed overnight at out of town locations. As the years went by, Sid was introduced to my brothers, Chuck and Dave, both LaSalle grad accountants. Chuck headed to Laventhol & Horwath before ending up in his own business, and Dave eventually joined our family firm. Sid also grew to know the rest of my siblings and my champion Irish Setters through our dinner table stories. To this day, he never forgets a detail and never fails to ask how things are for each of us.

In 1986, Dad was encouraging me to return to school for an MS in tax, but I had discovered a JD program at Rutgers School of Law in Camden, NJ that offered a tax certificate. I approached Sidney to help me decide between the two programs and graciously accepted his offer to write a letter of reference. Meanwhile, I had begun teaching review courses for the CPA exam, and Sidney was very excited to hear all about it.

Over the years, our family of accountants has learned tax history, the legislative process, tax theory and application, practice management, and business marketing "at Sidney's knee." His lessons have helped us to grow our firm and better serve our clients. Sid's insights made us more aware of the coming trends to our industry and helped us to better prepare for the many changes we have faced since 1969, when Dad attended his first conference at the Bellevue Stratford in Philadelphia. I am now teaching a variety of programs for Certified Financial Planner certificants. I make every effort to arrive early to make sure I am set up, and I stay late to answer all the questions. Like Sid, I jumped at the chance to learn the newest technologies, and I have taught online for nearly eight years.

Recently, I attended an Attorney-CPA (AAA-CPA) conference where Sidney spoke, providing me a brief chance for a face to face "hello." As always, his memory for the details of my family and our lives amazed me, but I truly appreciated the chance to thank him for all he taught us over the years. I can only hope to inspire my students as Sidney inspired me. Thank you Sid, you have been an inspiration to so many lives.

Changing the federal tax code after the Oakland fire

Robert L. Castle is a CPA in Oakland, California:

I first met Sid in the late 1960s, when I went to work for a very small CPA firm in Oakland, California. The big part of the practice was tax work. My boss suggested that I attend Sidney's seminars for both individual and corporate tax. At that first seminar, I was introduced to Sidney through a mutual acquaintance, and we struck up a lasting friendship.

In 1971, I decided to open my own practice. I called Sidney and told him what I was planning to do. He was kind enough to send me a number of materials that, to this day, I still use in my practice.

Sid's "whiz kids"

Through Sidney, I met Al Greenblatt, and Al and I became instant friends. We attended Sidney's tax workshops together, and one year we showed up wearing T-shirts that read "Sid's Whiz Kids" in blazing letters. The grin on Sid's face was a mile wide.

In the early 1970s, I became a single father, and I was raising a daughter. Sidney became a part of our family. He had dinner at our home every time he came to San Francisco. He watched my daughter grow as I watched his children grow.

The Oakland Hills Firestorm

In October of 1991, the city of Oakland sustained what to this day is the most costly wildfire in U.S. history: the Oakland Hills Firestorm. A total of 1,520 acres burned and 3,354 single-family homes and 437 apartments and condominiums were damaged or destroyed completely.[*] 25 of my clients were burned out in the fire.

In the aftermath, the city of Oakland set up a one-stop center where victims of the disaster could get assistance, and I stopped by to check it out. I happened to hear a young woman ask an IRS representative how much time victims had to use insurance money to rebuild without having to pay tax on the proceeds.

The agent basically told her not to worry about it. I thought that was the wrong answer. I grabbed an IRS code book that was sitting on a desk. Sure enough, Section 1033 at the time said that you had two years after receiving your insurance proceeds to rebuild, otherwise you had to pay tax on the proceeds.

I immediately realized that the time limit was a problem. I had a number of builders as clients, and they told me there was no way they could rebuild thousands of homes in two years and still handle their normal workload. To me, that was a signal that victims could not afford to rebuild because they would lose a third of their insurance proceeds to taxes.

I thought the time limit should be increased. I wrote a proposal to amend federal tax law to allow survivors in federally designated disaster zones to take up to four years to rebuild without being taxed on their insurance proceeds. Before going to his representatives in Congress with his proposal, he needed to get support for his idea.

---

[*] "Oakland Hills Firestorm 20th Anniversary is Reminder for All Californians to Get Prepared," News release, Property Casualty Insurers of America, October 19, 2011, www.pciaa.net/legtrack/web/ naiipublications.nsf/lookupwebcontent/9BD97F9123D349CC8625792E00786F5.

It happened that Sid was moderating an individual income tax seminar in San Francisco in December of 1991. Sid enthusiastically agreed to give Castle time to speak to the 1,100 CPAs in attendance. Castle explained the proposal and made a request of the CPAs: contact your clients and ask them to write their Congressional representatives in support of the proposal.

Later, Castle met with California Senator Dianne Feinstein to explain his proposal, and she assisted him in writing his proposal as a bill to be introduced in Congress. Senator Feinstein then arranged for Castle to meet with Senator Lloyd Bentsen, then the chairman of the Senate Finance Committee, to present the bill to him. With his support, the bill became law and is now known as Section 1033(h) of the Internal Revenue Code. Today, U.S. taxpayers in federally designated disaster zones have four years, instead of two, to rebuild their homes and businesses without having to pay income tax on the insurance proceeds.

"This gave victims of the Oakland fire an extra two years to get plans drawn, get approval of the city as well as the homeowners associations that were often involved, and get their homes and businesses rebuilt," Castle said. The law also benefitted the city of Oakland. If thousands of owners had not rebuilt, their properties would have been assessed as vacant land and at much lower values—and lower property taxes—than land with improvements. Today, in one Oakland neighborhood, homes that were valued at $70,000-$100,000 before the fire are now selling for $800,000-$1 million.

Castle's work in assisting his clients and others following the Oakland fire, and his success in getting the bill passed, has given him national prominence as a disaster relief specialist. When there is a federally declared disaster, he often gets calls from CPAs and others in the area asking for his help. "I am more than happy to share with them my experiences and give them the research tools they need to assist their clients."

"To Sidney, my thanks for helping to get this legislation passed to the benefit of all of Oakland's taxpayers. We owe you a deep debt of gratitude for helping us to rebuild our city to the wonderful place it is today."

"I always remembered the basic lessons of how to do your work"

Eli Weinberg is a retired partner of Lybrand Ross Brothers & Montgomery (now part of PricewaterhouseCoopers). He currently serves as treasurer of the Teagle Foundation, a not-for-profit organization devoted to working with colleges and universities to improve student learning through faculty involvement.

Every time I meet Sid Kess, I never fail to marvel at his energy and enthusiasm for what he is doing, especially when I realize he is probably 10 years older than me, and I'm 75 years old and feeling every bit my age.

I met Sid Kess over 50 years ago. I was a newly hired junior accountant at the firm of Lybrand Ross Bros. & Montgomery, now a part of PricewaterhouseCoopers. It was the summertime slow season in the accounting business, and all the young juniors were assigned to the typing pool to proofread

(continued on pg. 108)

(continued from pg. 107)
reports. I was lucky and was assigned to proofread the revised manuscript for *Montgomery's Taxes* that Sid was editing for the firm.

At the end of the day, the juniors would be complaining about the drudgery of proofreading, and I was having a wonderful time working with Sid, who always took the time to explain what he was doing, answer any questions, and seemed to be genuinely appreciative of my efforts, as if I was doing it as a special favor for him.

It was my introduction to the need for care, caution, but also creativity, in all aspects of my subsequent accounting work. I since went on to become a partner at what was by then Coopers & Lybrand, but I always remembered the basic lessons of how to do your work and how to deal with people that Sid Kess taught me.

Our paths have crossed many times in the intervening 50 years, and Sid has always been generous and enthusiastic about sharing his expertise with all who ask. Sid is a great human being; we should all try to emulate his good will and generous nature.

Sage advice

E. Martin (Marty) Davidoff is a CPA with E. Martin Davidoff & Associates in Dayton, New Jersey:

Not only has Sid helped me professionally, but his sage advice in other areas of my life has been candid, practical, and sound. In this day and age, how rare is it that someone calls me with the sole purpose of asking how I am doing? Sid does that regularly. Sid has accomplished in his career what nobody else I know will ever accomplish. Yet, he is just a regular guy, always willing to share. I love him for that as I am sure all of us do.

Professionalism and creativity

Owen G. Fiore, JD, Fiore WealthPlanningConsulting, Kooskia, Idaho:

I have known Sid for over 30 years, beginning when he brought me into his AICPA Tax Strategies conference and allowed me to provide input on the advisory board. At every conference with Sid, in every planning committee meeting with him as chair, I have seen his ultimate professionalism and creativity at work. He continues to amaze me with his energy and creativity applied to the tax profession.

On a personal level, Sid has been a friend to my wife and me, not only in good times, but when personal difficulties have arisen. What a wonderful and constant friend for us to have as we go through life.

"A True Gentleman and Friend"

Linda Hughes was a former manager in Instructor Recruitment/Professional Development at the AICPA:

Sid is someone I have the deepest respect for. He is a true gentleman and friend. During my one month hospital stay, Sid was one of the first persons to call me and wish me well. If there was anything he could do for me, just let him know.

A "rock star"

Rose Ann Beni is Sid's personal assistant:

I first heard of Sid while working at the AICPA, where he was considered a "rock star" among CPAs. But I didn't really get to know him until I became his personal assistant a short time ago. In the time I have known and worked with him, I've been impressed with his knowledge and genuine love of what he does, as well as his compassionate and caring nature.

Sid always thinks of others and how he can possibly help them. He is totally devoted to his family, as well as to friends and colleagues, whether he has known them for decades or for just a short time. If someone is in need, Sid's first thought is "what can I do to help?" Combining a love for his profession with an interest in those he interacts with on a daily basis makes Sidney the special person that he is. I have already learned many life lessons from Sid and look forward to learning many more.

Life lessons

Joseph W. Walloch, CPA, Walloch Accountancy Corporation, Redlands, California:

Sid has taught me many life lessons, the most memorable of which is the importance of family and friends. Sid has received numerous accolades, but Sid will tell you that their importance pales in comparison to the importance of family and friends.

Sid has embraced me professionally as well as embracing the "personal me" and my family, including my disabled son Greg, who has cerebral palsy and walks on crutches. Greg lives in New York and travels throughout the world performing his one man show, "White Disabled Talent," including a recent performance in Washington, DC with Academy Award winner Forrest Whitaker and Meghan McCain. Sid embraces Greg and helps him out on New York challenges when his California dad cannot be there. Sid shares his wisdom and advice, as well as generous acts of kindness to support Greg's career.

Thank you, Sid. My family and I are honored to be your friends.

Conclusion

If he were a different type of person, Sid's career might simply have been this: worked in public accounting as a director of tax and as a tax partner for many years, had a distinguished career, then retired.

But as everyone who knows Sid is well aware, there is much more to him than that. He chose to devote his tremendous talent, keen intelligence, and boundless energy not only to working in public accounting but also to helping others. He spent many years on the road, conducting his tax workshops, explaining new tax laws and rules in plain English, and offering practitioners practical advice on how to turn complex tax rules into revenue-generating opportunities. He conducted countless workshops for the AICPA, state societies, the UJA-Federation of New York, and many other organizations. Sid wrote books, articles, and columns and also created videos for practitioners and the public on taxes, estate planning, and many other topics. He assisted and collaborated with financial writers in writing articles and books. He assisted and encouraged CPAs and other professionals to develop their public speaking, teaching, and writing skills and to develop expertise in estate planning, pensions, state and local taxes, International Financial Reporting Standards, and numerous other areas. He helped them to apply their skills and expertise to build their reputations as continuing professional education

(CPE) teachers, find a career niche, change careers, expand their professional practices, or achieve other professional or personal goals. Sid offered innumerable ideas to people and organizations, including his courses and tips on preparing for the CPE examination, his tax tips column in the *New York Law Journal,* and his advice to practitioners on how to expand into financial planning services. The list is never-ending.

Now, more than 20 years after he retired from public accounting, Sid continues to lead a very active life. He is still conducting workshops and conferences; he is of counsel to a New York law firm; and he writes articles and serves as an editorial advisor to publications. He brings together people in need of jobs and employers in need of talent and takes every opportunity to encourage other professionals to do likewise. Sid continues to advise and mentor students, CPAs, and other professionals in their careers. He offers to help friends and, sometimes, people he has just met, deal with professional or personal issues. Above all, Sid is devoted to his family, and he reminds others that in the course of their busy lives, family comes first.

Sid's story does not have an end. It will continue in the teaching and writing of the CPAs, lawyers, and the myriad others who have learned from him, who help others as he has helped them, and who have the same passion for using their skills and talents not only to succeed in their careers but also to give back to their professions, their communities, and society. When they look back on their lives, hopefully, they will have the same sense of accomplishment and fulfillment that comes from having had rewarding careers and from having done some good in the world. And that will be Sid's legacy to those who come after him.

Bibliography

American Education Television Network

Products Authored or Co-Authored by Sidney Kess as of September 2003

Videos
Form 1040—An Update
> Observation: This video course was shown over a satellite throughout the U.S. It was the first attempt to develop continuing education for use in the home.

Books
Form 1040—An Update—Text
> Observation: This text accompanied the video course.

AICPA

Products Authored or Co-Authored by Sidney Kess. Partial Listing As of January 2012

For over 44 years, Mr. Kess conducted courses for more than 47 state CPA Societies and more than 725,000 practitioners. Each year over 25 Tax Return Workshops were conducted, reaching thousands of participants. At one time, one out of every four CPAs who attended an AICPA continuing education course attended a program that Mr. Kess personally taught. One out of every three CPAs used an AICPA course manual that Mr. Kess authored.

Books and Courses
Individual Income Tax Returns Workshop (47 years)
Corporate Income Tax Returns Workshop (46 years)
Accountant's Business Manual (with CD-ROM Toolkit)
Advising Clients in Tough Times
Kess on Tax Legislation 2010: Tax Relief Unemployment Insurance Reauthorization, and Job Creation Act
The AMT for Individuals: Strategy to Escape Its Reach (2 editions)
Paying for College: Tax Strategies and Financial Aid (2 editions)
Managing a Profitable Tax Practice (15 years)
Tax Research Methods and Techniques (15 years)
Tax Planning for the Closely Held Corporation (15 years)
Estate Planning and the CPA—Co-Authored
Avoiding Circular 230 Malpractice Traps and Common Abuse of Small Business Hot Spots
Sid Kess' Alternatives to Commonly Misused Tax Strategies: Insuring Your Client's Future
Tax Highlights for Individuals Update and Selected Review (1990)
Manual for Individual Income Tax Returns Video Workshop (33 years)
Manual for Corporate Income Tax Returns Video Workshop (32 years)
Manual for Current Tax Developments (1989, 1990, 1991)
Manual for Tax Planning Techniques for Corporations and Individuals (1989–1991)
Manual for Tax Planning for Businesses (1992)
Manual for Tax Planning for Individuals Course (1992)
Manual for Tax Developments for Business (1992, 1994)
Manual for Tax Developments for Individuals (1992, 1994)
Manual for S Corporations/Partnerships/LLCs Update Video Course (1993)
Manual for Tax Accounting Update Video Course (1993)
Manual for AICPA's Experts' Retirement, Insurance and Estate Planning Video Course
Manual for Employee-Independent Contractor Video Course
Manual for Revenue Reconciliation Act Video Course (1990, 1993)
Manual for AICPA's Experts' Tax Relief Act of 1997
Manual for Tax Planning for Corporations and Individuals: A Checklist Approach (1988)

Videos

Hundreds of thousands of CPAs have viewed Mr. Kess' videos during the past 36 years as a way of updating themselves for the tax season and to obtain Continuing Education Credit.

Individual Income Tax Returns Video Course (1972–2011)
Corporate Income Tax Returns Video Course (1972–2011)
Kess on Tax Legislation 2010 (On major tax bills, Mr. Kess prepares a video with a team of experts)
Current Tax Developments Video Course (1989–1991)
The AMT for Individuals: Strategies to Escape Its Reach (2004–2006)
Paying for College: Tax Strategies and Financial Aid (2004, 2006)
Tax Planning Techniques for Corporations and Individuals Video Course (1989–1991)
Tax Planning for Business Video Course (1992)
Tax Planning for Individuals Video Course (1992)
Tax Developments for Business Video Course (1992, 1994)
Tax Developments for Individuals Video Course (1992, 1994)
Questions and Answers on Individual Taxation
Questions and Answers on Corporate Taxation
S Corporations/Partnerships/LLCs Update Video Course (1993)
Tax Accounting Update Video Course (1993)
The AICPA Experts' Retirement, Insurance and Estate Planning Video Course
Employee-Independent Contractor Video Course
Planning for Older Clients Video Course
1990 Revenue Reconciliation Act Video Course
1993 Revenue Reconciliation Act Video Course
The AICPA Experts' Taxpayer Relief Act of 1997
The AICPA Experts' IRS Restructuring and Reform Act of 1998 Video Course
AICPA 2001 Tax Act Videocourse
2003 Jobs and Growth Tax Act
Tax Planning Techniques for Corporations and Individuals: A Checklist Approach (1988)

Newsletters

CPA Client Tax Letter (Editor)
CPA Client Bulletin (Editor)

AICPA National Tax Training School

Lectured at the AICPA National Tax Training School at
University of Michigan
University of Illinois

AICPA Tax Instructors Meeting

Mr. Kess organized and moderated several programs for the tax instructors for the AICPA Workshops on Individual and Corporate Taxation to guide them on techniques for more effective presentations. At his workshops, Mr. Kess personally instructed the leaders on more effective teaching techniques.

Tax Conferences

Thousands of practitioners have attended the annual conferences that Mr. Kess created and moderates for the AICPA.

Tax Strategies for the High-Income Taxpayer (created, organized and moderated the program for 26 years)

National Conference on Planning Strategies for Real Estate and Tax Advantaged Investments (2 years)

Sophisticated Tax Planning for Your Wealthy Clients (created, organized and moderated the program for 6 years)

Awards

2003 Special Recognition Award (for his many years of contributions to the AICPA Continuing Professional Education program)

AICPA Gold Medal Award for 2011 for distinguished service which is given to individuals who have made major contributions to the CPA profession and is the highest award granted to a CPA by the Institute.

AICPA created the Sidney Kess Award for excellence in continuing education to recognize individual CPAs who have made significant and outstanding contributions in tax and financial planning and whose public service exemplifies the CPA profession's values and ethics.

American Express

Products Authored or Co-Authored by Sidney Kess as of September 2003

Books

American Express Tax Guide (1998–2002)
American Express Quick-Prep Tax Guide (1999)

Baruch College

Products Authored or Co-Authored by Sidney Kess as of December 2011

Meetings

Guest speaker at California Alumni Meeting
Guest speaker at various student career meetings

Position

Adjunct Professor

Awards

Recipient of the Alumni Award for Outstanding Excellence In Career
Accomplishment

Honored by College for Outstanding Contribution to Field of Taxation

Outstanding Alumni Award in Field of Accounting

Boardroom, Inc.

Products Authored or Co-Authored by Sidney Kess as of December 2011

Tax Advisory Board

Chairman of the Tax Advisory Board for 15 years

Contributed articles and edit articles

Member of the Panel of Experts since inception of newsletter

Bottom Line Publications

Member of Panel of Experts—Taxes for *Bottom Line Personal, Bottom Line
Tomorrow, Bottom Line Business,* and *Boardroom Reports–Business*

CCH Incorporated

*Products Authored or Co-Authored by Sidney Kess. Partial Listing as of
December 2011*

Since the late 1960's, Mr. Kess' reporters, newsletters, CCH seminars, books,
courses, audiotapes and commentaries on every major tax act have reached
millions of CCH subscribers. Many of the books and audilex courses are
updated each year.

Awards

CCH's first lifetime achievement award for outstanding contribution to the tax
and accounting profession.

Tax Services

Financial and Estate Planning Reporter (4 volumes—since 1981) [Author and
presently Consulting Editor]

Business Strategies (since 1984) [Author]

Newsletters and Magazines

Estate Planning Review. (Created in 1974 and continued through 2010. Mr.
Kess was Consulting Editor)

Estate Planning Review—The Journal. (Estate Planning Review Letter merged
in an expanded Journal—Mr. Kess presently serves as Consulting Editor.)

Journal of Tax Practice and Procedure (Consulting Editor.)

Executive's Tax Review (1976–1984)

Tax Planning Review (1975–1993)

CCH Seminar Programs

Kess/Computax Seminar Programs (Organized CCH Computax User Conferences for 3 years)

Tax Strategies for High-Income Taxpayers

Books

Financial and Estate Planning Guide (16 editions) since 1976

1040 Preparation and Planning Guide (39 editions) [Now an electronic product]

1020 Preparation and Planning Guide [Now an electronic product]

706/709 Preparation and Planning Guide [Now an electronic product]

1041 Preparation and Planning Guide [Now an electronic product]

1120S, 1120 Preparation and Planning Guide [Now an electronic product]

1065 Preparation and Planning Guide [Now an electronic product]

Kess on Tax Legislation 2010: Tax Relief, Unemployment Insurance Reauthorization, and Job Creation Act of 2010

Kess on Tax Legislation 2009: American Recovery and Reinvestment Act of 2009

Kess on Tax Legislation 2004 Tax Legislation: Insights and Strategies

Kess on the Jobs and Growth Tax Relief Reconciliation Act of 2003: Insights and Strategies

Kess on the Job Creation and Worker Assistance Act of 2002

Kess on the 2001 Tax Legislation: Insights and Strategies

After the Crash: New Financial Planning Approaches

Employees vs. Independent Contractors: Problems and Resolutions

Family Tax Planning Post-Tax Reform

IRAs and Keogh Plans

New Family Wealth Transfer Opportunities

New Planning Opportunities and Pitfalls Under the Economic Recovery Act of 1981

New Planning Opportunities Under the 1984 Tax Law

Practical Guide to Individual Income Tax Return Preparation, 1973–1976 (4 editions)

Resolving the Fiscal-Year Dilemma

Retirement Planning After TRA '97

Retirement Planning Guide (7 editions)

Retirement Planning in Changing Times

Retirement Plans and Fringe Benefits After the Tax Reform Act of 1986

Tax Planning for Individuals and Small Businesses (2 editions)

Tax Planning Opportunities for Businesses Under ERTA

Winning Strategies for Business Under the 1986 Tax Reform Act

Winning Strategies for Individuals Under the 1986 Tax Reform Act

Winning Strategies for Individuals and Businesses Under the Revenue Act of 1993

Winning Strategies for the 90s: 1990 Tax Act and Beyond

Real Estate and Tax Shelters After the Tax Reform Act of 1986

Protecting and Preserving Wealth After the 2001 Tax Act: Practical Insights and Strategies from Leading Professional Advisors

CPE Courses/Audilex Tapes

Many of the audilex courses, such as the 1040 Preparation Course and the Corporate Income Tax Refresher Course have been updated annually since their inception in 1970.

1040 Preparation Course (annual since 1991—14 editions)

Accounting Methods (Learning Center Course)

Amortization Rules (Learning Center Course)

Auditor's Guide to Corporate Tax Planning (5 editions)

Annual Income Tax Highlights: What's New This Year for Individuals (3 editions)

Basic Law for Financial Planning

Business Tax Credits (Learning Center Course)

Charitable Giving Tax Strategies (Learning Center Course)

Corporate Income Tax Refresher Course—Form 1120 (annual since 1991—14 editions)

CPE Credit Service (bi-monthly since 1994)

Developments in Dealing With the IRS (CCH On-line CPE Library Course)

Developments in Light of INDOPCO (CCH On-line CPE Library Course)

Developments in Valuation (CCH On-line CPE Library Course)

Education Tax Incentives (Learning Center Course)

Employees vs. Independent Contractors

Estate Planning Course (5 editions)

Estate Tax Preparation Course (4 editions)

Federal Tax Audio Advisor (bi-monthly since 1991)

Fiduciary Income Tax Course (annual—3 editions)

Financial and Estate Planning Course (5 editions)

Financial and Estate Planning Quarterly (quarterly since 1974)

Final Regulations on Required Minimum Distributions (Learning Center Course)

Fundamentals of Partnership Taxation (7 editions)

Fundamentals of Pension and Profit-Sharing Plans, Including 401(k) Plans (10 editions)

Gifting As A Tax Strategy (Learning Center Course)

Guide to Corporate Tax Planning (10 editions)

How to Prepare for the CPA Exam (10 editions)

Individual Income Tax Refresher Course—Form 1040 (annual since 1970—34 editions)

IRAs and H.R.10 (Keogh) Plans (10 editions)

IRS Interest on Overpayments and Underpayments (CCH On-line CPE Library Course)

Kess on Financial and Estate Planning: A CPE Course (3 editions)

Partnership and Limited Liability Income Tax Refresher Course—Form 1065 (annual since 1993—12 editions)

Estate Planning Course (annual since 1977)

Estate Tax Preparation Course (4 editions)

Partnership Income Tax Refresher Course (7 editions)

Pass-Through Entities Income Tax Refresher Course (annual since 1996)

Pension and Profit-Sharing Course (10 editions)

Personal Residence As A Tax Shelter (Learning Center Course)

Personal Tax Credits (Learning Center Course)

Retirement Planning in Changing Times

Roth IRAs (CCH On-line CPE Library)

S Corporation Income Tax Refresher Course—Form 1120S (annual since 1971-1995 – 24 editions)

Special Rules For Disabled Individuals (Learning Center Course)

Tax Considerations In Starting A Business (Learning Center Course)

Tax Related Birthdays (Learning Center Course)

Tax Decisions on Qualified Retirement Plans and IRAs on Death (CCH On-line Library Course)

Tax Views (monthly since 1972)

Writing Off Start-Up Expenses and Paying Employment Taxes (CCH On-line CPE Library Course)

CPE Courses/Audilex Tapes: Tax Legislation

For more than 40 years, analyses of every major federal tax bill have been prepared on audiotape and with an accompanying manual. Since the 1997 Tax Act, a CPE course in print form has been prepared on any major tax legislation.

Explanation of the Tax Reform Act of 1969

Security Transaction Under the Tax Reform Act of 1969

Effect of the Tax Reform Act of 1969 on Moving Expenses

Employer Plans Under the Tax Reform Act of 1969—Lump Sum Distributions, Restricted Stock and Stock Options

Real Estate Under the Tax Reform Act of 1969

New Depreciation Changes Under the Tax Reform Act of 1969

Trust and Estate Planning Under the Tax Reform Act of 1969
Revenue Reconciliation Act of 1971: Explanation & Analysis
1974 Pension Reform Act: A New Challenge
Explanation of the Tax Reduction Act of 1975
Tax Reform Act of 1976: Explanation and Analysis
Estate Planning Strategies Under the 1976 Tax Reform Act
Revenue Act of 1978: Explanation and Analysis
Estate Planning Implications Under the Revenue Act of 1978
Tax Act of 1981: Explanation and Analysis
Estate Planning Implications of the 1981 Tax Act
Tax Planning Opportunities for Business Under ERTA
Tax Act of 1982: Explanation and Analysis
Tax Act of 1984: Explanation and Analysis
Tax Reform Act of 1986: Explanation and Analysis, Including Planning
    Strategies
Retirement Planning and Employee Benefits Under the Tax Reform Act of
    1986
Real Estate and Tax Shelters After the Tax Reform Act of 1986
Revenue Reconciliation Act of 1987: Explanation, Analysis and Planning
    Opportunities
Technical Corrections Act of 1988: Explanation and Analysis, Including
    Planning Strategies
Revenue Reconciliation Act of 1989: Explanation, Analysis and Planning
    Opportunities
Revenue Reconciliation Act of 1990: Explanation, Analysis and Planning
    Opportunities
Alternative Minimum Tax Course
Kess on the 1997 Tax Act: Insights and Strategies
Retirement Planning After TRA '97
IRS Restructuring and Reform Act of 1998 (CCH On-line CPE Library
    Course)
Kess on IRS Restructuring and Reform: A CPE Course
Kess on Taxpayer Relief Act of 2000
Kess on 2001 Tax Legislation: A CPE Course
Kess on the Job Creation and Worker Assistance Act of 2002
Kess on the Jobs and Growth Tax Relief Reconciliation Act of 2003: Insights
    and Strategies Course
Kess on Tax Legislation 2004 Tax Legislation: Insights and Strategies
Kess on Tax Legislation 2009: American Recovery and Reinvestment Act of
    2009
Kess on Tax Legislation 2010; Tax Relief, Unemployment Insurance
    Reauthorization, and Job Creation Act of 2010

Current Courses in CCH Learning Center

(These courses are electronic segments of the various books that are updated as well as the focus of each of the Audio Advisor issues.)

1040 Preparation and Planning 1: Fundamentals (2012 Edition)

1040 Preparation and Planning 2: Gross Income (2012 Edition)

1040 Preparation and Planning 3: Deductions (2012 Edition)

1040 Preparation and Planning 4: Tax Computations and Credits (2012 Edition)

1040 Preparation and Planning 5: Acquisition and Disposition of Property (2012 Edition)

1040 Preparation and Planning 6: Deductions for Business and Other Special Deduction Rules (2012 Edition)

1040 Preparation and Planning 7: Special Tax Computations (2012 Edition)

1040 Preparation and Planning 8: Special Problems (2012 Edition)

1040 Preparation and Planning 9: Tax Practice (2012 Edition)

1041 Preparation and Planning 1: Tax Fundamentals for Trusts and Estates (2012 Edition)

1041 Preparation and Planning 2: Income and Deductions (2012 Edition)

1041 Preparation and Planning 3: Tax Computation and Completing the Return (2012 Edition)

1041 Preparation and Planning 4: Schedule K-1 (2012 Edition)

1041 Preparation and Planning 5: Special Situations (2012 Edition)

1065 Preparation and Planning 1: Tax Fundamentals (2012 Edition)

1065 Preparation and Planning 2: Income and Deductions (2012 Edition)

1065 Preparation and Planning 3: Schedules and Completing the Return (2012 Edition)

1065 Preparation and Planning 4: Special Situations and Planning (2012 Edition)

1120 Preparation and Planning 1: Introduction to Form 1120 (2012 Edition)

1120 Preparation and Planning 2: Income (2012 Edition)

1120 Preparation and Planning 3: Deductions (2012 Edition)

1120 Preparation and Planning 4: Tax and Payments (2012 Edition)

1120 Preparation and Planning 5: Estimated Taxes and Special Topics (2012 Edition)

1120S Preparation and Planning 1: Tax Fundamentals (2012 Edition)

1120S Preparation and Planning 2: Business Income, Deductions and Tax Payments (2012 Edition)

1120S Preparation and Planning 3: Schedule K (2012 Edition)

1120S Preparation and Planning 4: Other Schedules and Tax Planning (2012 Edition)

706 Preparation and Planning 1: Tax Fundamentals (2011-2012 Edition)

706 Preparation and Planning 2: Property of the Decedent (2011-2012 Edition)

706 Preparation and Planning 3: Debts of Decedent (2011-2012 Edition)

706 Preparation and Planning 4: Credits and Deductions to the Estate (2011-2012 Edition)

706 Preparation and Planning Part 5: Special Situations and Completing the Return (2011-2012 Edition)

709 Preparation and Planning: Completing the Gift Tax Return (2011-2012 Edition)

Alternative Minimum Tax for Individuals (Fifth Edition)

American Recovery and Reinvestment Act of 2009

Amortization Rules (Third Edition)

Asset Protection and Risk Management for Individuals and Businesses

Bankruptcy Act of 2005

Business-Related Tax Credits

Buying and Selling a Home

Education Tax Incentives: Opportunities and Strategies (Sixth Edition)

Emergency Economic Stabilization Act of 2008

Estate and Gift Tax Planning Today (Second Edition)

Financial and Estate Planning Documents (Second Edition)

Gifting as a Tax Strategy (Third Edition)

Home Sales and Foreclosures: Tax Breaks and Alternatives

Investments After the Tax Relief Act of 2010

Kess on Tax Legislation 2009: American Recovery and Reinvestment Act of 2009

Kess on Tax Legislation 2010: Tax Relief, Unemployment Insurance Reauthorization, and Job Creation Act of 2010

Paying for Long-Term Care

Recent Tax Developments (January–February 2011)

Recent Tax Developments (July–August 2011)

Recent Tax Developments (March–April 2011)

Recent Tax Developments (May–June 2011)

Recent Tax Developments (November–December 2011)

Recent Tax Developments (September–October 2011)

Recent Tax Penalties

Roth 401(k)s (Second Edition)

Small Business Jobs Act of 2010: Tax Rules

Tax Breaks for Going Green (Third Edition)

Tax Changes Under Health Care Reform

Tax Considerations in Closing a Business

Tax Credits for Individuals

Tax Implications of Debt Forgiveness

Tax Issues For Owners of Commercial Property

Tax Rules for Charitable Contribution Deductions

Tax Strategies for Employees and Business Owners in a Tough Economy (Second Edition)

Tax Strategies for Sideline Businesses

Tax Treatment and Strategies for Windfalls

Roth IRAs (Fourth Edition)

CPA Magazine

As of December 2011

Magazine

Since 2004, Mr. Kess has been the Executive Editor of *CPA Magazine*. As a result of Mr. Kess' efforts, several outstanding practitioners who focus on their area of specialty have been brought in. The publication is one of the top tax magazines for accountants.

Honors

In 2006, Mr. Kess was selected as the "most influential practitioner" by *CPA Magazine*.

Campbell University

Products Authored or Co-Authored by Sidney Kess as of December 2011

Conferences

For more than 25 years, Mr. Kess has lectured for Campbell University at an annual meeting for CPAs, attorneys, bank trust officers and financial planners on Update On Individual Taxation. These sessions were recorded and played over the radio, pointing out tax highlights for the general public.

Lectures
For over 25 years, Mr. Kess has lectured to the student body in a general session on careers, goals, family and lifetime challenges.

Position
Adjunct Professor

Awards
Campbell University has funded the Sidney Kess Trust Scholarship for outstanding trust majors.

Comprehensive CPA School

Products Authored or Co-Authored by Sidney Kess as of September 2003

Books
Self Study Guide for Preparing for the CPA Exam in Theory (Annual)
Self Study Guide for Preparing for the CPA Exam in Law (Annual)
Self Study Guide for Preparing for the CPA Exam in Problems (Annual)
Self Study Guide for Preparing for the CPA Exam in Auditing (Annual)
Selected Material for the CPA Problems Exam-Questions-Study Material-And Other Practice Aids (Annual)
Shortened CPA Review for the Taxation Portion of the CPA Exam (Annual)
Kess and Gross Shortened CPA Business Law Review
How To Prepare For The CPA Exam

Courses
For 18 years, Mr. Kess conducted the leading CPA Review Course in Problems. More than 20,000 CPA candidates attended the course in New York.
Conducted Problems Review Course (1957–1975)
Conducted a short review course in taxation (1957–1975)
Conducted a shortened review course in law (1957–1975)
How To Prepare For The CPA Exam
Ran meetings for various states, including NY, California & Texas
Lectured to CPA candidates, including the Association of CPA Candidates, on How To Prepare For The CPA Exam

Evoke

Products Authored or Co-Authored by Sidney Kess as of December 2011

Courses
Kess' 1996 Individual Tax Update
Tax and Financial Strategies for the High-Income Individual

Books

The text for the two above cited courses was on a CD-ROM disk and was one of the first innovative programs involving programmed instruction for teaching taxes.

Fidelity Investments

Products Authored or Co-Authored by Sidney Kess as of December 2011

Videos

The 30-Minute Tax Break—Finding Shelter Under the New Tax Law (1993

Grosset & Dunlap

Products Authored or Co-authored by Sidney Kess as of December 2011

Books

Preparing Your 1040 Form (1982–1984)—by Robert Metz & Sidney Kess

H & R Block

Products Authored or Co-Authored by Sidney Kess as of December 2011

Books

Technical Editor of TAX PLANNING ADVISOR (A Year-Round Approach to Lowering Your Taxes This Year, Next Year and Beyond)

Lybrand

Products Authored or Co-Authored by Sideny Kess as of September 2003

Tax Courses

Tax Principles Course
Tax Savings Check List Course
Estate Planning Course
Tax Planning for the Closely Held Business—(Annual)
CPA Preparation
Lectured to staff on how to prepare for the CPA exam
Authored "Shortened CPA Tax Course"
Authored the following self-study guides for preparing for the CPA exam:
    Theory
    Practice
    Auditing
    Law

Books

Contributor to Montgomery's Federal Taxes

Main Hurdman

Products Authored or Co-Authored by Sidney Kess as of December 2011

Mr. Kess was National Director of Taxes for Main Hurdman from 1969–1985. His responsibilities included supervising the tax practice activities of 87 offices throughout the United States.

Books

Estate and Financial Planning—Some Essentials (3 editions)

National Association of Estate Planners & Councils

Positions and awards as of December 2011

Positions

National Chairman of Estate Planning Awareness Week (October 2009)
National Co-Chairman of Estate Planning Awareness Week (October 2010)

Awards

Estate Planning Hall of Fame (2007)
Hartman Axley Lifetime Service Award in Recognition of Distinguished Service to the Estate Planning Profession and the National Association of Estate Planners and Councils (2009)

New York Law Journal

Products Authored or Co-authored by Sidney Kess as of December 2011

Column

For 43 years, Mr. Kess has authored a bi-weekly column on "Tax Tips," continuing through the present time. More than 1,000 articles have been published.

New York State Society of CPAs

Products Authored or Co-Authored by Sidney Kess as of December 2011

For over 45 years, Mr. Kess' lectures and workshops have been the most widely attended CPE courses conducted by the New York State Society of CPAs. Thousands of students have attended his popular annual tax workshops.

Courses

Find Your Tax Answers Faster
Managing An Effective Tax Package
Individual and Corporate Tax Returns Workshop (39 years)
Jobs and Growth Tax Act of 2003

Conferences

Spoke at the annual summer conference at Briarcliff

Moderated Elder Law Conference in New York City and Rochester

Luncheon speaker at Estate Planning Conference

Moderated a series of conferences on "Will the CPA Survive The Next Century?" (NY State preview of the AICPA Vision Project)

Joint sponsorship of program on Section 529 with TIAA-CREF

Organized and moderated a series of three post-election planning conferences (2009–2010)

Moderated breakfast briefing session

Committees

Member of the Nominating Committee

Member of the Tax Committee

Award

Recipient of Hall of Fame Award (2009)

New York Times

Products Authored or Co-Authored by Sidney Kess as of December 2011

Books

Your Guide to Preparing 1980 Returns (February 1981)—A collection of 12 articles written with Mr. Kess' assistance.

News Articles

Annually since 1967, Mr. Kess has assisted editors in preparing annual guides to preparing tax returns. He has been a consultant to Bob Metz, Deborah Rankin, Gary Klott, Fred Andrews, Jan Rosen, and Leonard Sloane

For years the *New York Times* would consult with Mr. Kess about what was new during the year, and they would prepare a series of articles that were written with his assistance to acquaint the readers with what is new in preparing their tax returns. Each year Mr. Kess has assisted the editor in charge of developing the Sunday Supplement in the Business Section of the *Times*. These *New York Times* interviews were often reprinted in numerous newspapers around the country and reached millions of people.

PESI

Products Authored or Co-Authored by Sidney Kess as of December 2010

From 1997–2010, Mr. Kess has conducted Update programs in approximately 10 cities throughout the country.

Books

The Taxpayer Relief Act of 1997 and Individual Income Tax Update—by
 Sidney Kess

Individual Income Tax Strategies and Preparation—(1998–2000)

Tax Act of 2001: Explanation, Analysis and Planning Opportunities

2002 Individual Income Tax Preparation: An Update After the Job Creation &
 Worker Assistance Act of 2002 and the Tax Act of 2001

Professional Educational Network

Products Authored or Co-Authored by Sidney Kess as of September 2003

At the initial stages of the introduction of Professional Educational Network,
the president to the U.S. audience, consulted with Mr. Kess regarding various
aspects of the course content, marketing strategies, possible people to
interview, etc.

Videos

Individual Update 1992–1994—(CPE Network)

Tax Management (BNA)

Products Authored or Co-Authored by Sidney Kess as of September 2003

Books

A Practical Guide to Tax Planning (1974) by: Sidney Kess & James Cheeks

Find Your Tax Answers Faster (3 editions)

UJA-Federation

Products Authored or Co-Authored by Sidney Kess as of December 2011

Mr. Kess originated and moderated The New York Estate, Tax & Financial
Planning Conference for 43 years. It has served as a model for hundreds of
charities throughout the country. Millions of dollars in charitable gifts have
indirectly been raised from this program.

Conferences

Created and moderated the New York Estate, Tax & Financial Planning
 conferences (43 years)

Created and moderated conference on Retirement Planning, Elder Law and
 Charitable Giving (13 years)

Organized several conferences on What Every Woman Should Know About
 Her Husband's Affairs (10 years)

Moderated several programs with Blanche Etra and Claire Vogelman for
 women who are major donors to the UJA-Federation

Created and moderated conference on Elder Law (3 years)

Created and moderated conference on Charitable Giving (3 years)

Moderated conference on Estate & Retirement Planning in Staten Island (2 years)

Moderated conference on Estate & Retirement Planning with Brooklyn Bar Association (jointly sponsored with UJA-Federation)

Moderated joint conference with Richard Eisner & Company on the 2001 Tax Legislation

Satellite Programs

Meeting in West Palm Beach for Prospective Donors

Participated in the Westchester Annual Conference

In Home Programs

Spoke at the homes of major donors of the Women's Planned Giving Committee

Awards

The Sidney Kess Award for Professional Excellence in the Philanthropic Environment

Warren Gorham & Lamont

Products Authored or Co-Authored by Sidney Kess as of December 2011

Newsletters

Kess Tax Planning Report (1972–1985)

Kess Accounting Practitioner's Report

Books

The Tax Reform Act: A Manual for Practioners—by Sidney Kess

Kess: The Tax Reform Act—Manual for Tax Practitioners (1969)

How the Tax Reform Act Affects Banks & Financial Institutions—Edited by Sidney Kess

The Kess Tax Planning Manual (1970–1971)

The Kess Tax Planning Manual—Planning Under the Tax Reform Act (1971–1972)

The Kess Tax Planning Manual (1972–1973)

Conference Programs

Conference on The Tax Reform Act of 1969

Conference on Accounting & SEC Developments 10 Years After The Accounting Principles Board Was Organized

Administration

Assisted in the introduction of Arthur Rosenfeld, who was hired and ultimately became President of Warren Gorham & Lamont. Arthur was able to build up the Warren Gorham & Lamont book division to the point where WG&L had become one of the leading tax text publishers in the country.

Wealth Advisors

Products Authored by Sidney Kess as of December 2011

Web Seminars

Each year, for the past five years, Mr. Kess has done a year-end planning web seminar with Robert Keebler.